KU-532-677

RHP

WORLD YOUTH GAMES

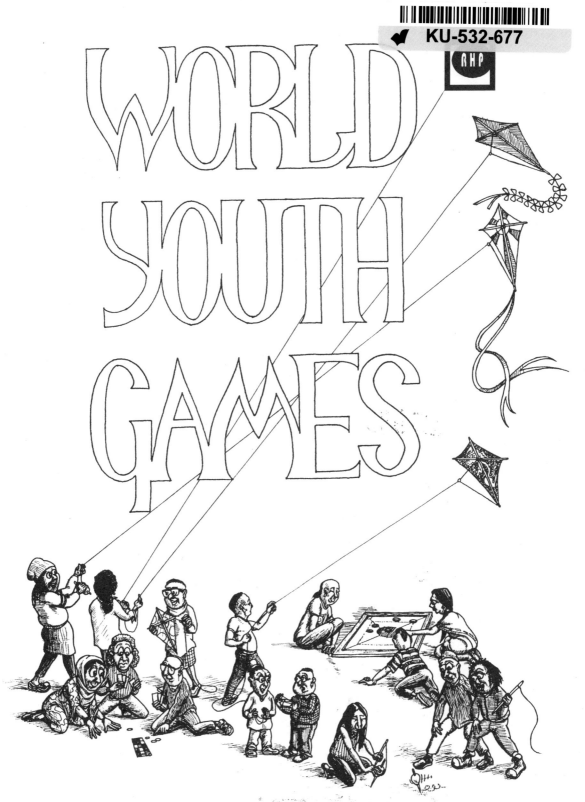

Alan Dearling and Howie Armstrong
with cartoons by Gubby

First published in 1995 by

Russell House Publishing Limited
38 Silver Street
Lyme Regis
Dorset DT7 3HS

© *Alan Dearling and Howard Armstrong 1995*

Cartoons by Gubby
Diagrams by Gubby & Alan Dearling

All rights reserved. No part of this publication may be reproduced, stored in a retrieval system or transmitted in any form, or by any means, electronic, mechanical, photocopying, recording or otherwise, without the prior permission of the Copyright owners and the publisher.

Photocopying Permission
Permission is given by the authors and the publishers for photocopying material in the games, as indicated in the text, by organisations purchasing the book.

British Library Cataloguing-in-Publication Data:
A Catalogue record for this book is available from the British Library.

ISBN 1-898924-50-3

Printed by:
Hobbs the Printers
Totton,
Hants.

LEEDS METROPOLITAN
UNIVERSITY LIBRARY
1702035438
HJ-BU
7454 14.7.98
DISCARDED
790.083 DEA

Contents

Acknowledgements
Chapter One   *Introduction   1*

Chapter Two   *World of Youth Games   7*

Chapter Three   *World of Activities   55*

Chapter Four   *World of Relationship Games   95*

Index   139

LEEDS BECKETT UNIVERSITY
LIBRARY
DISCARDED

ACKNOWLEDGEMENTS

The trouble with acknowledgements is that you always forget someone! Anyway, with a certain amount of temerity, here goes. We'd like say an especial thanks to various friends at Candolim in Goa - they know who they are; likewise to a number of writer colleagues including the Nikitins from Russia, Karl Rohnke from America, Robin Dynes, Alan Smith and Sue Jennings from the UK. A number of individuals have also helped us with specific games ideas, they include: Himu Gupta, Tom Brean, Sunita Arora, Douglas, an Indian gentleman originally from Calcutta and now at Boots HQ in Nottingham (Alan's lost his surname), Jenny Nemko, Billie and Alex Wilcox, John McWhirter, Naomi Leigh at Just Games, Hannah and David Jacobs, Ron Higgs, Gail and Russ Caddy, Mihai Rosca and Radu Sabau from Romania, Alan Burton, Makhdoom Ahmad Chisnti, Estelle and Symphony from Lyme Regis PO, Nigel Clarke, Communicado Theatre Company, all the staff and kids at Panmure House (past, present and future), Claudia Beamish and Michael Derrington, Spaska Malinova in Bulgaria and Geoffrey Mann.

Gubby deserves a special thanks for enlivening these pages with his own inimitable brand of what he calls 'doodles from the pit.' You have to know Gubby to picture exactly what he means, but in the meantime we'll leave it to your imagination!

As ever, we had the support from our partners, kids and work colleagues in putting up with us and helping to put the piles of bits of paper into some semblance of order. They also suffered and at times hopefully enjoyed being guinea pigs in testing out games and activities. We'd particularly like to thank Tracey Hunter, Janey, Christine Harding, Antony, the Jones family and the regulars at various hostelries in Lyme Regis where some of the pub-related games were re-launched. Also, a thanks to all our other Russell House colleagues for thinking that the book was worth publishing.

We also gratefully acknowledge the many other games-players and writers who we have plagiarised (nicked stuff from)! Few games are truly original, and many in this collection are hand-me-downs over many generations. Our hope is that the users of this book will help to preserve that continuity of sharing by passing on the rules and the enjoyment of games to succeeding generations.

Alan Dearling and Howie Armstrong
June 1995

INTRODUCTION

Introduction....2

Major benefits from use of games....3

How to use this book....4

Who you can use games with....4

Planning for games sessions....5

Organisation of this book....6

WORLD YOUTH GAMES

INTRODUCTION

The idea for compiling *World Youth Games* arose directly as a response to requests from some readers of the *New Youth Games Book* and its predecessor the *Youth Games Book.* We were told that there was:

♦ a demand for more games, sequences and activities;
♦ and that many user groups would like to have games which related to particular countries and cultural traditions.

We saw this as an interesting challenge. We contacted many of our colleagues around the UK and in a number of other countries both in Europe and throughout the world. We also scoured new and second hand bookshops, occasionally wincing as we had to put our hands into pockets for very expensive reference tomes. Additionally, we had stockpiled a good supply of games and techniques which had not been used in the many editions of the games books we had previously produced. Finally, and providing lots of fun, we used every opportunity when we were travelling about in a whole variety of places from Greece to Goa, Italy to the Netherlands, Brussels to Hungary and Romania, and Scotland to Wales, to pick the brains of our hosts and find out what games they remembered playing when they were kids.

What you now have in your hands is the fruits of that labour. It isn't, and cannot be, comprehensive. Hopefully it does provide an interesting and imaginative collection of activities which can enhance any youth club, school, social work group or family get-together. Twenty years of writing about, and even longer playing games, has taught us a few things. You cannot legislate for how 'other' people will use the material you share with them. Nor can you provide a very exact guide to the length of time which should be allowed for using a particular sequence, or the age group/ability level of the group with whom the game is to be used. Instead we try to make helpful suggestions on how games can be used and the type of situations and pitfalls which may arise.

We have done our best to gather together a rich and varied collection of games, many of which are in danger of being lost, as the TV-watching generations evolve into games machine playing, CD-book readers. A lot of cultural traditions are in danger of becoming history. If this book helps to keep that history alive as a living organism, then we make no apologies. We hope though that it is more, and can be a practical

and fun collection which can remind adults of relatively simple pastimes which serve
to:

- encourage adults and young people to play together as a shared activity;
- provide an opportunity for creative play;
- remind players that games are part of a verbal and participatory tradition which comes from many cultures throughout the world;
- value and support the individual involvement of everyone involved in the games;
- provide opportunities to learn new skills, numeracy and literacy, and the value of rules and boundaries in normal life;
- offset the effects of adherence to rigid 'curriculum dominated' activities, and the deficits created by social and cultural deprivation;
- mix non-competitive and competitive opportunities for active participation;
- encourage relationship building.

Much of the value of games participation, which we suggest applies for adults, are also the benefits for children and young people. Robin Dynes ('Creative Games in Groupwork. Winslow Press'. 1990) and Karl Rohnke (many books on games activities in the USA, including, 'Silver Bullets'. Kendal/Hunt 1984) are two of the world's games gurus. We would agree with the kind of benefits list that they claim for the use of games and activities with young people. We have made up our own list based on our experience and what Karl and Robin see as:

Major benefits from the use of, and involvement in games:

- personal growth; being all you can be;
- self-confidence; being capable and competent;
- a sense of personal worth; being able to value oneself;
- encourage involvement; taking part is more important than success or failure;
- motivation; new interests and potential activities for personal leisure time with friends;
- stimulation for creativity and imagination;
- increased understanding of other people's needs;
- mutual support within group situations;
- increased social interaction skills;
- literacy and numeracy skills;
- stimulation for physical and mental skills and co-ordination;
- confidence in being able to trust other people both physically and mentally;
- willingness to accept responsibility and take risks;
- stimulate an interest in one's own cultural identity and the cultures of other people and countries;
- improve decision-making;
- aid the mutual support of members of any group;
- promote empathy, sensitivity and understanding between people;
- develop trust of others;
- help people to gain their identity;
- develop physical and mental dexterity and agility;
- encourage the enjoyment of games and activities as a natural and creative part of growing up;
- have fun and enjoyment;
- relax and learn strategies to cope with personal problems.

HOW TO USE THIS BOOK

Being fifteen years 'longer in the tooth' than when we compiled the original 'Youth Games Book' we now realise that the people dipping into this book can be virtually anyone.

Who you can use games with
The types of work we have personal experience of games and activities being used in include:

- running youth centres and youth groups
- youth social work and intermediate treatment
- probation work
- informal groups of young people
- family groups
- work with Travellers
- child protection and therapy
- adventure and activity group work
- counselling and encounter groups
- holiday courses
- recreation programmes
- play work and adventure playgroups
- residential centres
- New Games sessions
- church and religious groups
- school and college classrooms
- uniformed youth organisations
- hospitals and specialist care settings
- training groups for young people and adults, especially of the 'leader training' type
- business organisation training sessions
- coffee bars, pubs and leisure settings
- professional training courses for social workers and youth workers
- family homes.

It's a long list, but we suspect it still only reflects a fraction of the situations in which games may be played. Given the diversity of the people and places, we have decided in this book to keep the professional 'jargon' to a minimum. We have already listed how we think games can provide positive experiences for young people and can enhance various types of group activities. We also hope that this book may be 'culturally friendly' for users who may be reminded of games which are half-remembered or long forgotten friends!

For other users, we have tried to present enough information about the rules, equipment and settings in which games take place to enable you to 'have a go' at most of the games. We have ourselves used games and activities in an extremely wide range of places, from inside a tipi in a woodland festival site; to a psychiatric hospital; through to summer playschemes in inner cities; programmes to tackle offending behaviour, and one night a week youth clubs in draughty village halls. We hope there is something here for all of those settings and more besides!

Where specialist equipment is required there are often options involving a bit of handicraft work or experimenting with available materials. Wherever possible we have also tried to point out where users need to be especially sensitive when using activities which some individuals may find too difficult or personally stressful.

Planning for games sessions

Planning for games sessions can be very important in many groupwork settings, so we would urge games session organisers to try out games themselves before using them with groups. It is also important to view the material in this book as a flexible resource.

Do try to:

♦ consider what is suitable and appropriate for your participants;
♦ encourage your group to modify rules and make up their own adaptations of games and activities;
♦ use games as a way of building and improving relationships;
♦ utilise games as a resource which involves adults and young people participating together;
♦ be aware of issues to do with race, gender, impairment and sexuality as they occur in games sessions, and use the opportunity to combat stereotyping and discrimination.

Most of all, we hope that you find this collection stimulating, fun to use, and a useful resource for all your games sessions. In using the games you will be helping to keep a long cherished tradition of games playing alive. In the words of the New Games players from America:

PLAY HARD - PLAY FAIR - HAVE FUN

Organisation of this book

Following on from this introduction, the book is organised into three main sections. They are:

The World of Youth Games which includes table games, board games and less active sequences which are representative of many different countries ranging from Africa to India, North America to China, Europe through to England, Ireland, Scotland and Wales. Caroms rub shoulders with Dreidles, Crag, Put and Take, Pachisi, Tarrocco, the Nikitin materials, Squails and the Dictionary Game.

The World of Activities brings together more active games and sequences, including playground games, outdoor sequences, and group recreations and puzzles. Included in this section you'll find Gooly Dunda, States' Shuffleboard, Ring Games, Fighting Kites, Kabaddi, String figures, Horseshoes, Longy-Della, unusual Hopscotch variants, Battling Tops and Treasure Hunts.

The World of Relationship Games offers a wide variety of games and sequences for use in groups where adults are trying to enhance young people's self-confidence and social, linguistic and numeracy skills. They can help in the development of trust and improve mutual understanding. The games and sequences include 'ice-breakers,' 'physical trust games' and larger scale, group participation events. The section includes; Wordles, Messages, Speakeasy, Human Train, Your Number's Up, Pack Your Bag, Personal Shields, Sex Roles, Rivers, Frankenstein and Cat and Mouse.

WORLD OF YOUTH GAMES

Forehead Game....8
Black....8
Polish Draughts....9
Fan Tan....10
Put and Take....11
Nikitin Materials....12
Tangram....14
Dice Games....15:(Beetle16; Martinetti 17; Crag 18; Hearts 19)
Dreidles....19
Ring Games....20:(Ringboard 21)
Old and Antique Board & Table Games....21
Puzzle Time....23:(Knee Bends 23; Glass Trick 23; Palindromes 24; A Fishy Match 25; Dotty 25; Match This 26; Lateral Problem 26)
Playing Cards....26
Tarrocco....28
A Few Card Games 30:(Slapjack 30; Le Vieux Garcon 31; Happy Families 31; Go Boom 32)
Hand Games....33:(Hei Tama tu Tama 33; Tippet or Up Jenkins 34)
Number Pairs....34
Pachisi....35
Game of Books....36
Dots and Lines....38
Inventing a Game: Bert's Gate....38
Spellicans....44
Caroms....44
Squails...46
Planks....47
Dictionary Game....48
Mancala Games....50:(Awari 50)
Scrabble Variations....51:(5 Start 51; Bonus Point 52; Double Bag 52; Recycler 52; Solo 52)
Jewish Passover: Festival of Freedom....52
Curved Ball....54

FOREHEAD GAME

This peculiar word game for between four and six players originated in America and was introduced in the American magazine 'Word Ways' by Dave Silverman in 1973. For use with groups of young people it is only suitable when all of the players have a reasonably large knowledge of words with four letters (as opposed to four letter words)!

Each player requires a small slip of paper, spare paper for notes, a pen and a piece of masking or scotch tape. **Play** begins with each player writing a word with four letters onto their slip of paper. They then fix this to the forehead of the person on their right.
- Each player sees the words of their opponents, but not their own, which they have to try and guess during the course of the game.
- In turn, players can either:
    -make up and announce a word with one letter from each of the words they can see on the foreheads;
    -guess at the word on their own forehead.
- No new word using letters from the available foreheads may be used more than once.
- It's a good idea to have a dictionary on hand to settle spelling arguments.
- You must decide whether a player leaves the game (and their word) if they make a wrong guess. With youthful players, we'd recommend that they remain in until someone guesses their word and that round of the game ends.

It's an odd game and one you may want to experiment with by changing the rules around a bit.

BLACK

The 'Black' in the title relates to the name of the person who invented this little paper and pencil game. It's different than many we have played and introduced to youth groups - we hope you enjoy it too! It is designed for two players, but by using a larger playing board can be adapted for three and four players. Coincidentally, we own a commercial version of the game which was marketed as 'Nile',

To start off you need a square or rectangular grid of smaller squares. You might like to enlarge and photocopy the one on the next page. We found playing on a ten by ten square gave about the right length of line and contortions. It can be played by youngsters from about eight upwards, since there are not many rules.

Play starts with a board set out like this:

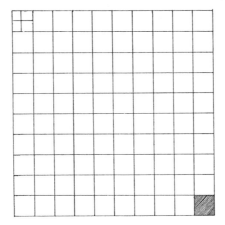

The bottom right hand square, which is shaded, is the area players are trying to reach with the line they are constructing.

- Players take turns to draw one of the three sets of marks into a square which extends the continuous line.

- The player who starts must use the cross shape in the top left hand corner of the board.
- If a player joins the line to the edge of the board they lose the game.
- If a player manages to join the line to the shaded area they win.
- The line may cross over itself.

And that's about it! A different game to pass the time and one with enough lateral and spatial thinking that it does include an educational element.

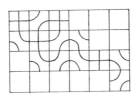

POLISH DRAUGHTS

We've not included ordinary draughts in this or the *New Youth Games Book.* We have assumed that if you and your younger friends can play draughts you might like a more challenging alternative. Almost every European country has its own version of draughts. Out of Spanish, German, Russian, Turkish and Polish draughts, this is the version we find most challenging. It was invented about two hundred and fifty years ago by a Pole living in Paris. It can be played by most people from about nine or ten years of age upwards.

One of the only drawbacks is that you need an extra large board with one hundred squares on it and each player has twenty pieces. As in draughts the pieces start off on the black squares and can only move onto other black squares.

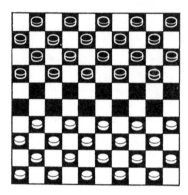

Play involves:

- Pieces moving one square forward in a diagonal direction.
- Pieces can take those of the opposing colour by hopping over them either in a forwards or backwards direction.
- Pieces can take more than one enemy piece at a time, and if they land on the last row they are crowned king (by placing a second piece on top of the first). However, if they can take further pieces in the same move they must do so and do not become king on that turn.
- As in English draughts, a player must take a piece if they are able to do so. If there is a choice of pieces to take, they must take the king rather than an ordinary man if they have the option. If the opponent points out a move where the player could have taken a piece, they must then make the taking move.
- When a piece becomes a king, unlike in ordinary draughts, it can move as far as it wants in any diagonal line **and** travel as far beyond that piece as it wishes.
- If a king is taking a number of pieces in the same turn, it must not jump over the same opposing piece more than once, but may travel over empty squares more than once.
- The winner is the person with only their pieces left on the draught board.

FAN TAN

Essentially this is a gambling game, but it can be played for points instead of money if you are using it with young people. It is arguably the most popular game played in China and in Asian communities throughout the world.

It is a game for four players, plus a banker, in the version we offer here. On the streets of China it is played with a banker and as many people who want to gamble. The banker usually keeps 25% of the stake money.

To play you need a small jar of beans or pebbles and a square table. Each corner of the table is designated 1, 2, 3 and 4. In the children's version each player owns one of the numbered corners. The banker then places a random number of beans into a bowl and then proceeds to take out one, two, three and then four beans, continuing to do this until there are four or less beans left in the bowl. Whichever number of beans is left, say three, determines the winner.

In another **version** the banker always takes the beans out in groups of four, using a small stick to rake them into groups. The groups of four beans are disregarded until the last batch which determines the winning number.

For playing with young people, we awarded one point to the winner of each round, with the overall game being one when one player reaches ten points. In the adult game, the banker shares out the total amount bet, less their 25%, between the those who bet on the winning number.

PUT AND TAKE

Played with small tops, also known as teetotums, this is a simple, but fun gambling game which can easily be adapted for playing with counters. Its origin is uncertain. Alan was given a put and take top by his grandmother when he was about five years old. She told him that the tops had originally been made by soldiers in the trenches during the first world war. This sounds plausible, since they are small, and easier to play with than a pack of cards. Other books claim it as an American game. Apparently in the 1940s it was very popular across the United States, but too many 'loaded tops' brought the game into disrepute!

We have certainly enjoyed sharing the game with young people and it is an ideal group game when camping or sitting in a coffee bar. To play, you require a six or eight sided top. If you can't locate one in a second hand or antique shop, it is quite easy to make one out of wood, or even out of a soft metal such as brass.

The layout for the six sided top is:
1) Take one   2) Take all   3) Take two   4) All put   5) Put two   6) Put one
and on the eight sided top:
1) Put one 2) Take one 3) Put two 4) Take two 5) Put three 6) Take three 7) All put
8) Take all

You require at least three to play, and it works best with about five or more players. To start everyone puts in one counter or coin into a central pool. Then, players take turns to spin the 'put and take' top, each following the instructions on the uppermost side of the top when it stops spinning. For instance, if you get an 'all put,' everyone puts in one more token. Play continues in the round until either someone gets 'take all,' or the pot runs out. It sounds boring, but we assure you that it is fun and gets quite exciting as the pot grows and no-one gets the 'take all.'

THE NIKITIN MATERIALS

Almost by chance we came across a range of very interesting materials and child development theories from Russia. A mutual friend in North London knew that we were compiling the new book and put us in contact with Aleksey Nikitin. Aleksey is the eldest child of Boris and Lena Nikitin. He was the first 'guinea pig' in his parents' personal experiment to evolve a fresh insight into children's development. Their ideas and the materials they used to help their own children develop their capacity to learn were viewed in the USSR as a challenge to the orthodoxy of the State educational and medical systems. The Nikitin's first book, 'Are we on the right track?' came out when Aleksey was two years old. It immediately became a popular classic - the second edition was banned by the Russian authorities!

The Nikitin's house became a kind of shrine of alternative schooling, visited by over 1,500 visitors a year, and bombarded by thousands of letters from parents, teachers and medical practitioners. By 1972, Boris and Lena had a family of seven children who were brought up in a flat on the parents' joint income of 200 roubles a month, at a time when even the official State figures recommended a subsistence level of 50 roubles per person per month. The Nikitins kept on developing what they called their 'Development Games,' which were used by each of their own children in turn. They also continued writing up their theories and accounts of their own experiences. Literally millions of copies of their books sold in the USSR, many illicitly, and nearly all heavily censored, while the State withheld any income from their labours.

Their most popular title, 'We and our children' was translated into German and Japanese in the 1980s. The Nikitins had thought that the problems they perceived in the State education system in Russia were unique; the responses to their books in Japan and Germany proved them wrong. People everywhere feel that 'restrictive education' systems confine and can delay the development of the individual child. The books, including 'The gifted child: not a gift of nature' and 'The Creative Ladder' which explains the use of the range of the Nikitin developmental games and adds, what the Nikitins called 'A bit of theory', have subsequently sold hundreds of thousands of copies. A full version was finally published in Moscow in 1991, with a much expanded range of 'tasks' for children to attempt.

Only now, and in a very limited way, are the UK public becoming aware of the Nikitin's theories of child development and the potential for using their games materials in child development, either in the family home or social welfare/education settings. Aleksey is living in North London and the games and a monograph version of the 'Creative Ladder' are now available.

The Materials

In the 'Creative Ladder' Boris Nikitin offers a description of the Nikitin 'Development Games':

"1) Each game consists of a set of tasks which is solved with the help of cubes, building blocks and various shapes made of card or wood.

2) The tasks are set in different forms, such as models, pictures or drawings, or instructions either written or verbal. This acquaints the child with the diverse methods of transferring information.

3) As is common with traditional games, the tasks are arranged in approximate order of increasing difficulty.

4) The tasks have a very wide range of difficulty, from those achievable by a 2-3 year old up to those which most adults would find taxing.

5) The slow increase in difficulty of the tasks enables the child to progress and to improve their abilities without anyone's help. This contrasts with standard educational practice in which everything is explained and controlled, thus fostering only the executive abilities."

We have had the opportunity to use the first two sets of the Nikitin's materials: the Magicubes and the Multi-cube. The other sets are: Quadrats (an extension of Chinese Tangrams) Building Blocks (model building from plans or imagination) and the Geocube (rather like a coloured, cubic version of what was once marketed in the UK as the L-Game).

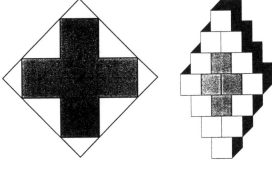

Magicube   Multi-cube

In use, the Magicube and Multi-cube are a cross between a Rubik-cube and a jigsaw. One of the major appeals is that they have lots of solutions, not just one. The accompanying booklets offer coloured patterns to construct with the cubes. Some are easy, some are difficult. Having encountered a number of puzzles, they are not unique, but are certainly good examples of materials which can help children learn through:
-problem solving

-manipulation of objects using physical and mental dexterity
-personal exploration.
The Nikitins stress that use of the games must be considered relative to the difficulty of the task and the ability of the child; that prompting should be avoided, as should ridicule or 'putting down', and that games should be fun and part of the natural "easygoing freedom" of childhood development.

We do not find either the games or the theories expounded in the 'Creative Ladder' radical. They offer commonsense suggestions of how adults can nurture the development of the child through creative and stimulating challenge and play. For us, it was interesting to see that such materials were first produced at a time of repression in the USSR. In a strange way, perhaps it parallels the search for alternatives in learning and teaching methods by many teachers, parents and child development workers in the UK, who feel that *education* is more than a National Curriculum, and that flexibility of approaches to learning are a key to true social and academic education.

Resources
Magicubes (£24.95), Multi-cube (£29.95) and the Creative Ladder (£4.95 or £3.95 if purchased with a book) and other Nikitin materials are available from NBA Technical Services, 481 Caledonian Road, London N7 9RN.

TANGRAM

This is reputed to be one of the oldest puzzles or games in the world, originating from China, where it was called 'Chi' i shiso pan,' which translates as the 'Wisdom Puzzle.' In the sets you are most likely to find in the West there are seven pieces which can be made by cutting them out of card. There is also a much rarer and more complex, fifteen piece Tangram set. If you have a photocopier, you can copy/enlarge the diagram below either straight on to card, or use paper, glue and card to construct one or more Tangram sets. A good size for a set is a 10cm square. Sets can also be bought from some games shops.

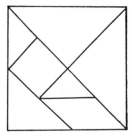

The aim of Tangram is to solve particular problems or to use the imagination to invent new shapes and designs. The rules are very simple:
- In every shape all seven pieces must be used.
- Each piece must be placed next to another and never overlap.
- The aim is to either construct geometric shapes or silhouettes.
- The player can try to find ways to make shapes such as those given on this and the next page, or can invent new shapes.
- When using a number of Tangram sets with a group of young people it can be fun to organise races to see who can be the first to make up a particular shape.

Try to make:
Geometric shapes:

Silhouette shapes

Believe us, they are all possible, but not easy! When Napoleon was in exile he spent much of his time creating new shapes with a seven piece Tangram set. Now it's up to you and your young friends.

DICE GAMES

Alan is the proud owner of a rather wonderful Roman dice which was originally used as a spinner. His friend Carla found it on an archaeological dig in Italy and was kind enough to give it to him as a present. Unlike our present dice it had a hole through it to take a sharpened stick. Dice with six and eight sides which are spun are usually known as *teetotums.* It is very easy to make a simple version of a spinning dice by drawing and cutting a six-sided piece of card marked with one to six, then putting a hole through the centre to take a pencil, which is used as the spinner.

Even earlier, the knucklebones of dogs and sheep were tossed to determine what action to take or not take. In the UK, dice have six sides, usually with smoothed off corners, and each side has a pattern of dots (or pips) on it denoting a value between one and six. All dice (or die) were traditionally called the Devil's Bones, alluding to their Pagan ancestry. During childhood, young people use them for race and board games as a means of controlling the movement of playing pieces. Snakes and Ladders, Ludo, Backgammon and Monopoly are four well known and loved board games requiring dice for moving playing pieces around. However, both in the UK and throughout the world, they are essentially a means of gambling. Pachisi is described elsewhere in this section of the book. It is the ancestor of Ludo. During the 2nd World War, American prisoners of war sent literally thousands of requests for Pachisi sets to the Red Cross. These were dutifully supplied, but officials later found those same sets and the playing pieces, but the dice were being put to other uses!

Travelling around the world, dice games using all shapes and kinds of dice and spinners abound. Because most of them are pure gambling games, we have limited our descriptions to a couple of interesting ones, plus a couple of very unusual variations. There are also a lot of games which use special dice, which can be bought or made. These include:

Crown and Anchor *(three dice, each marked identically with the four suits and a crown and an anchor)*
Poker Dice *(five dice, each marked identically with Ace down to the nine of a suit)*
Owzthat *(a cricket game which utilise two special cylindrical dice, each with six sides)*
Golf Dice *(uses five dice, which are thrown in a specific colour order to replicate the playing of each hole at a golf course)*
The Game of Pigs *(uses two plastic pigs as dice which can land on their feet, back or sides)*
Schimmel, or Bell and Hammer *(originally from Germany, uses eight special dice and five cards. The dice have a Bell or a Hammer on each one.)*

Beetle

This is a game which can be purchased as a commercial boxed game, but it is a simple paper and pencil game which has been enjoyed by young people for at least a couple of centuries. We cannot find out where abouts in the world it originated from, but we found early examples in both American and British books published at the end of the nineteenth century.

The game can be played just about anywhere between two and six players. Each player needs a paper and pencil, and one ordinary dice is required, or you can make up a special 'beetle' dice with the six sides marked as follows (or use an ordinary dice with the numbers in brackets representing the various parts of the beetle's anatomy.):

B=body(1); H=head(2); L=legs(3); E=eyes(4); F=feelers(5); T=tail(6)
To draw a complete beetle, each player needs to get one 1, one 2, two 3s, two 4s, six 5s, (sometimes reduced to two 5s, one for each set of three legs), and a single 6.

Play begins with each player throwing the dice once in each round. To start their drawing of the beetle, each player must begin by throwing a B or 1 for the body, which they then draw. Subsequently, a player can add tail, legs of head, but not feelers or eyes if the head hasn't been drawn on the body. The first person to complete their beetle gets a score of thirteen points (one for each part of the beetle) and the other players total up their scores on the same basis of the number of limbs they have completed.

For a brief period of time in the 1950s the game was a craze in the UK and 'Beetle Drives' were held in community halls, in much the same way as Bingo is organised today.

Martinetti

This one is also known as Round Dozen, Centennial and Ohio, depending upon which country you are in. It proved popular with young people we played it with. You need three dice to play. Two or more players can play Martinetti, which also requires one board, drawn up on a sheet of paper or card as follows:

1	2	3	4	5	6	7	8	9	10	11	12

Each player requires a different counter to show their position in the game.

Play begins after deciding who will go first. The aim is to become the first player to move their counter from one to twelve and back again. This is accomplished by throwing three dice in a turn. To get the playing counter onto the board, the player must throw a one. However, unlike in Shut the Box and other dice games, the three dice may be used to score a number of separate moves in a single turn. It's not that complicated, so read on! For instance, if a player starts by throwing: 1,2 and 3, they can move:

- 1=square 1
- 2=square 2
- 3=square 3
- 3+1=square 4

- 2+3=square 5
- 1+2+3=square 6.

Players do not need to use the score on every dice they throw.
If a player fails to notice a number they can score, then the next player can 'use' that number on their next go. The game finishes when the first player returns their counter to square number one, having successfully scored all the numbers on the board.

In essence it is a mixture of a racing game and shut (close) the box, which we have described in the *New Youth Games Book*.

Crag

This is also known as 'Cheerio' with very slight variations on the scoring rules. It requires three dice and can be played by anywhere between two and a dozen players. It is quite similar to the commercially marketed game of 'Yahtzee', so you can save yourself, or your organisation a few pennies by learning the relatively simple rules.

By drawing out the following table you are half way to understanding the game. Rather obviously you need as many columns across the top of your score sheet as there are players.

POINTS	DICE VALUES	ALAN	HOWIE	CHRISTINE	TRACEY
ONE EACH	1s				
TWO EACH	2s				
THREE EACH	3s				
FOUR EACH	4s				
FIVE EACH	5s				
SIX EACH	6s				
ODDS (20)	1,3,5				
EVENS (20)	2,4,6				
LOW STRAIGHT (20)	1,2,3				
HIGH STRAIGHT (20)	4,5,6				
THREE OF A KIND (25)	3 OF A KIND				
THIRTEEN (26)	TOTAL 13 WITHOUT DOUBLES				
CRAG (50)	TOTAL 13 INCLUDING A DOUBLE				
TOTAL					

Players take it in turns to throw the three dice and may then re-throw one, two or three dice for a second time. The aim is to make an entry in one of the columns. In thirteen rounds, each player must make an entry for each section, even if it is a zero. The number thirteen has special significance, and high scoring potential in this game.

For instance, if a player throws: 1,1,6 they might throw the 6 again to try and get three ones, or throw one 1 and the 6 again, to try and get a low straight, which scores fifteen. The winner is the person with the highest score at the end of thirteen rounds.

Hearts

This is a nice simple game which can be played with a special dice set of six dice, each marked up as follows:

Each player throws all six dice in their turn, and only one dice of each letter scores, as follows:
- 5 points for an H (even if they have more than one H)
- 10 points for H,E
- 15 points for H,E,A
- 20 points for H,E,A,R
- 25 points for H,E,A,R,T
- 35 points for H,E,A,R,T,S

If a player throws three Hs, they lose all their score to date.

The first player to reach a score of 100 wins the game.

It should be quite easy to buy blank dice, from a specialist games store, which can be marked up with the letters which form the word HEARTS.

DREIDLES

The spelling of these four-sided spinning tops, which originated in medieval Germany, is a matter of some dispute! Our friend, Jenny Nemko, who works for the Beeb, insists that they are spelled as above, but the Encyclopaedia Judaica spells them 'Dreidls' and in America they are called 'Dreiduls.' Their name is pronounced 'drey-dull.' Despite their German origins, they are best known as a Jewish game. It has an unusual history. At many times during their history the Jewish people have been persecuted, and they were forbidden to practise Judaism. To disguise their religious meetings, they sometimes had children on hand playing with the small dreidles. If intruders interrupted a meeting, the elders immediately became engrossed in the children's games. Traditionally, Jewish children were only allowed to play games during the festivals of Chanukah and Purim by the rabbis.

Nowadays the dreidle is still played with, and is especially associated with the Hanukkah (sometimes spelled Chanukah); the Festival of Lights. The dreidle has the hebrew letters

N,G,H and S inscribed on its four sides, which stand for the words:

Nes Gadol Hayah Sham

meaning 'A great miracle happened here.' The miracle happened in 165 B.C.E. (Before the common era) when a Jewish group called the Maccabees were besieged by the Syrians in the Temple of Jerusalem. They had an oil lamp with only enough oil left for one day. Somehow the lamp continued to burn for eight days until reinforcements arrived. The playing of dreidles and the lighting of the Chanakiah - an eight stemmed candelabra, celebrate that victory during the Festival of Lights.

Children usually play with a dreidle while the candles are burning, using counters, nuts or sweets for stakes, but the original German game was used for gambling. In the last two centuries dice were regarded as sinful in many cultures, including in Britain, because they were used in gaming, and various forms of spinners were used in a variety of games as an alternative. (Put and Take is described earlier in this chapter.)

A dreidle made of plastic or metal, often brass, can be bought, but it is also easy to make one from wood. You need a cube about one centimetre square. Paint or letraset the hebrew letters on the four outer sides, then carefully drill a hole in the centre where a dowel can be inserted. This should fit tightly and be sharpened to a point about one centimetre below the cube. Hardwood is best for the cube, so that it doesn't split.

N =]

G =]

H = ה

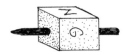

S = ש

The rules of the game are simple. Players sit in a circle and all put in two coins or counters in to a pool to start. The first player spins and if:
- it stops with an N facing up, they do nothing;
- it stops with a G facing up, they take all the pot, and everyone puts in two more coins to start a new sequence;
- it stops with an H facing up, they take half the pot, and everyone puts in one coin to the pool;
- it stops with an S facing up, they all put one coin in to the pool.

It is a very easy game to learn and since the playing piece is small, it fits easily into the pocket. We have found that spinner games are very popular with most children.

RING GAMES

These days ring or hoop throwing seems to be banished to the fairground and the larger amusement arcade, but that wasn't always the case. For generations up until about the second world war, throwing six rings at a Ring board, sometimes known as 'Hoopla' or the 'Hoop game,' was a very popular recreation. Until the 1930s, some historians of pub games claim that the Ring board game was actually more popular than Darts. No-one seems to know for sure where the game originated, but County Cork has claimed it as its own. In the next chapter of the book we describe the closely related games of Quoits and Horseshoes, which are played out of doors.

Ring board

We have both bought and constructed boards in the past and it has proved popular with young people, since it is a bit easier to play than darts and has less potential for lethal damage! Boards are easy to make and are usually diamond or shield-shaped and between 16" and 18" high. There is no definitive set of rules for playing the game or for the layout of the board. However, most games that we have come across use six rubber or plastic rings of between three and four inches diameter. Below we show the layout of three different boards.

 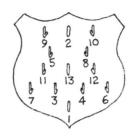 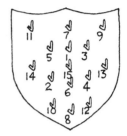

Play in most versions of the game is either between two or three individuals or between teams of equal numbers.

- Each player throws their six rings at the board and scores the total of the rings which catch onto the hooks.
- The game is won by the first player to reach a score of 121, and it is usual for players to have to get the exact score to finish.
- In some places, three rings on a single number wins the game outright.

A **variation** is to play 'Round the Board' which involves players throwing each number in the correct order, 1,2,3,4 etc.. In this game two rings on a single number count as a double, so two 4s give a score of eight, and the player then throws at the number nine.

OLD AND ANTIQUE BOARD & TABLE GAMES

The art of discovery

As games players, forgetting the bit about being authors and youth and community workers, we have found that some of our favourite games have been unearthed in the dusty back rooms of junk shops, antique showrooms and occasionally friends' attics. Even if it means that we face more competition, we would highly recommend the 'search and discovery' aspects of hunting out old games. It is something akin to being an amateur detective. Not only do you have to find the games, you frequently then have to find out how they might be played and what pieces are missing! As well as being enjoyable to play, many of the older games are collectors' items, so, on occasions you may want to think twice before letting them suffer the throes and ravages of the local youth club. You won't find one, but the oldest games ever found in the world come from Egypt, Ur and Palestine and date back to approximately 4,000 BC.

Types of games

Because we have tried to enthuse members of our own families in the delights of games playing, our choice of games-to-buy is curious, individual, and not entirely connected to play with young people. Over the years we have picked up a vast range of items ranging from 'Put and Take' tops mentioned in this chapter, through to double twelve sets of 'Dominoes' (definitely unwieldy!), Tiddledy Winks' (their original name from the end of the nineteenth century), table top 'Croquet', old ball bearing maze puzzles such as the 'Silver Bullet,' which chronicles action from the front during the First World War, unusual sets of playing cards from Russia and Japan and a whole host of boxed games. Who remembers Waddington's 'Astron-a trip to the stars,' or their 'Railroader' game, where you have to build a railroad through North America? Or, how about the thoroughly enjoyable 'Peter Rabbit's Race Game', (based on Beatrix Potter's creations) which we believe is still available in reproduction form?

Playing Crokinole at a games session

However, our favourite games over the years have tended to fall into the 'table game' category, rather than board games. In different houses, flats and clubs we have had a full size bar-billiards table, an old French 'Bagatelle' board (which is a game played with a cue), a 'Pachinko' machine from Japan, which is related to our amusement arcade machines where you flick a ball-bearing around a vertical board - in the Japanese version you put ball-bearings into the machine instead of coins, and it pays out in ball-bearings! We still have an interesting collection of table games which are the forerunners of the pin-ball machine. They tend to be garish, brightly painted, and involve propelling marbles and ball bearings around various courses. Amongst others we have 'Klimit', which replicates the first round-the-world air race, starting from *Croydon* airport in Britain; 'Big Shot' and 'Manual Kick Back' which are developments on from Corinthian Bagatelle.

Finally, we have a few very solid (literally!) board games like 'Niner' which is an elastic propelled shuffleboard; the Dutch shuffleboard game 'Sjoelbak' which resembles the marbles 'Archboard' game played with wooden disks on a polished board; 'Puffball' where participants blow a ping pong ball across the round table; Table Skittles (also known as Bar Skittles or Devil amongst the Tailors) and 'Crokinole', which was originally a Canadian game, and Merilyn Simonds Mohr describes as:

> *"a bit like marbles brought indoors and made adult and respectable with its own polished wooden board and flattened round playing pieces, instead of skittering glass balls." (*The Games Treasury. 1993. Robert Hale Ltd)

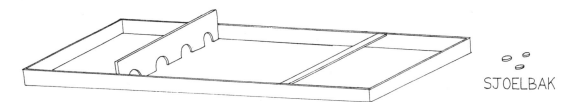

SJOELBAK

You may find that the young people in your life like particular types of games, for instance using Tarot cards, playing boxed board games, or using the more active table games such as 'Shove Ha' penny.' As with our section on making your own games, we are suggesting that the 'hunt' can be an activity in itself, and if you carry this out with a small group of young people you can help them to appreciate the historical aspects of playing games.

PUZZLE TIME

When we were compiling the original 'Youth Games Book' in 1979 one of the things that struck us was the tremendous interest young people have in puzzles, tricks and problem-solving. To further encourage this, we offer here a range of diversions which should amuse, confuse and hopefully entertain. In terms of their origins, the majority are from American and UK sources, though some of them date back to the late nineteenth century.

Knee Bends

Women are more supple than most men and this little exercise will prove it. Ask participants to stand with their toes against a wall, then take exactly two steps backwards so that they are two feet away from the wall. Now they should be invited to bend from the waist and place their forehead against the wall. Up to this point they can use their hands, but now they have to let them hang loose.

The challenge is to see if they can now stand back upright without using their hands. Not many men can do this, whereas many women find it relatively easy.

Glass trick

A lot of tricks which are performed are based on a small bit of manipulation. This is a classic example. To start you require three identical glasses which you set up like this:

The challenge is to move two glasses at a time, and in three moves have the glasses all the same way up. The answer is as follows:

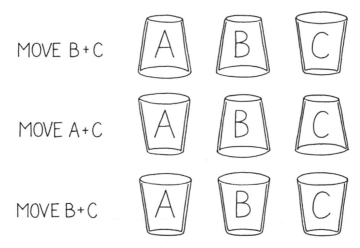

MOVE B + C

MOVE A + C

MOVE B + C

Now comes the sting in the tail. You invite anyone else to do it and you turn over the centre glass B so it is lip down. Now the fun begins. However hard your challengers try to repeat your feat, they are bound to fail. It's a cheat, but an amusing one!

THEIR SET UP

Palindromes

Words which spell the same forwards and backwards are called palindromes. There are quite a lot of them in the English language. Because they are a little odd they are fun to play around with. Below is a short quiz, the answers to which are all palindromes.

1. A popular type of stock cube.
2. A polite way to address a lady.
3. Adam and .....
4. You look through it.
5. To flatten something.
6. Mid-day.
7. Sparkling drink.
8. A posh reception given by the council.
9. A female sheep.
10. A small measure of alcoholic drink.

Answers

1. Oxo
2. Madam
3. Eve
4. Eye
5. Level
6. Noon
7. Pop
8. Civic
9. Ewe
10. Tot

A Fishy match

There are a large number of puzzles using matchsticks. This one is a bit more unusual than some.

Start off with eight matches arranged to make a fish shape. Then challenge the onlookers to make the fish swim in the opposite direction by moving only three matches.

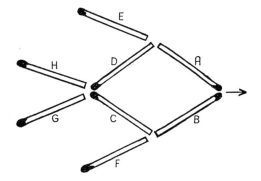

The answer is to move matches 'A,' 'E' and 'H' to new positions.

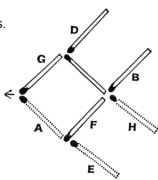

Dotty

In this one the challenge is to place eight dots onto the diagram so that there are two dots on each straight line and two dots on each circle.

And the answer:

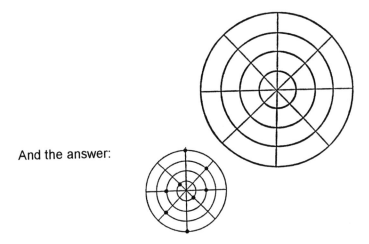

Match this!

This is a game which is a puzzle. It requires little equipment. Each player needs a square marked out on a piece of paper in the following manner. They each also require five coins.

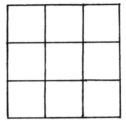

The aim is to match the position of the coins set by the person organising the game. To start, all the players have their eyes closed and the organiser places their five coins in any of the nine squares. When they call "look," all the players study the placement of the coins, while the organiser counts to ten out loud. The coins are then covered with a piece of cloth and the contestants try to set out their own coins in the same pattern. When they have had a go at this, the original coins are uncovered and anyone who has matched them correctly scores a point. Players can take turns to be the organiser. Playing the game up to ten points usually keeps people amused for about twenty minutes.

A lateral problem

Lateral thinking problems are very popular with adolescents and even some adults! Here is a typically devious one. The idea is for the person telling the following story to then be questioned by the participants giving the answers: "Yes, no or irrelevant." In this way the questioners gradually move towards the correct answer.

A man and his son go out on a fishing trip. The father was drowned after an accident, but the son lived and was rushed into hospital for an operation. The old surgeon looked at the young man and said, 'I can't operate on him, he is my son.' How can this be true?

The answer is that the surgeon was the young man's mother.

PLAYING CARDS

Including more information on card games, might at first glance, seem a waste of space in this book. But, we would urge you to read on. Some of the information we unearthed about the cultural identity of playing cards, where they may have come from, how they developed, and something about the special significance they have for some people, struck us as being very interesting and we thought that we'd share a bit of our newly acquired knowledge. What is more, almost all young people throughout the world have played with packs of cards at some time in their lives, even if it is only to build fragile, 'house of cards' structures. Perhaps they too would like to know more about the bit of history that they are playing with......................

A bit of history

We are pretty convinced that modern day playing cards are a corrupted form of the original cards known as the Book of Thoth, named after an Egyptian god, roughly corresponding to Mercury. The cards were originally used for the purpose of divination,

or more accurately were meant to show symbolically, man's relationship with the universe. The symbols shown on the Tarot pack's 56 court and pip cards (also known as the minor arcana) are divided into four suits. The Tarot suits represent the four elements:
Fire (Wands, Batons or Clubs) - Water (Cups) - Air (Swords) - Earth (Disks)

In modern packs, the four suits in the UK are depicted as Hearts (which correspond to cups); Spades (which were swords mis-translated from the Spanish-Italian word *espadas,* or the old English word *spados,* both meaning swords); Clubs (wands or batons), and Diamonds (disks, coins or deniers, denoting wealth). Along the way, the French used the trefoil plant instead of the club symbol, and for a time, German packs used Hearts, Acorns, Bells and Leaves for the four suits. It was the French who threw out the Valet or Page cards, reducing the minor arcana of the Tarot pack down to 52. However, 'Tarochino' is an Italian game played with a shortened Tarot set of 62 cards, and throughout Europe and in Mexico card games using the Tarot pack are still played using 54 and 78 cards (the full fortune telling pack). To confuse things more, Italian, German and Spanish packs sometimes omit eights, nines and tens, leaving 40 cards in the pack, and the French Piquet pack has just 32 cards, including nothing lower than a seven. Modern Swiss and older German packs sometimes consist of 36 cards, omitting the twos, threes, fours and fives. For patience games, solitaire packs which are about half the normal physical size, are easier to use on a table top, and are more suitable, anyway, for younger children.

No-one knows who invented playing cards, but Gypsies are credited with using the Tarot pack and the ordinary pack for fortune telling, and for spreading their use from Africa and possibly India, throughout the states of Europe. The earliest cards now in existence are dated as having been painted in Italy in 1352.

What a lot of people don't realise (us included, until we were researching this book!) is that there are at least two levels of 'meaning' hidden in the Tarot and the conventional packs of cards. The Tarot pack has 78 images which are pictorial versions of the Qabalah or Cabala, which is known as the Tree of Life. This is sometimes referred to as the *Yoga of the West* and is a complex, obscure and secret body of knowledge and ideas. Controversially, it combines the traditions of Jewish mysticism (particularly the

Hekhaloth) and writing, with the occultists' model of the Tree, which represents all the relationships between the universe, man and God. It was all a bit too much for our little brain cells, but it did give an interesting twist to the notion that cards are an instrument of the Devil, which was St Bernard of Siena's view in a sermon in 1423.

The other aspect of cards and their origin which may be of some interest is the design of the court cards. Our cards are based on a French design of about 1480, which has been amended through time, principally changing the clothing to match the court of Henry VIII, rather than the Renaissance. The figures on the cards actually represent real people, or figures from myths and legends:
King of Hearts: Charlemagne
Queen of Hearts: Judith from the Bible, or Helen of Troy
Jack of Hearts: La Hire, from Joan of Arc's Council of War
King of Spades: David
Queen of Spades: Pallas, a Greek goddess
Jack of Spades: the French hero, Reynaud
King of Diamonds: Julius Caesar
Queen of Diamonds: Rachel
Jack of Diamonds: Hector de Maris, half brother of Lancelot
King of Clubs: Alexander the Great
Queen of Clubs: Hecuba, a queen in Troy and mother of Paris
Jack of Clubs: Lancelot

Quite an interesting and ill-assorted collection!

Repeatedly throughout history, there have been purges to try and remove the images of royalty from playing cards. In the French Revolution, the Commune decreed that all the royal cards were banned and they were replaced with images of Sages and Geniuses, Virtues and Seasons, Heroes and Workers. It was Napoleon who re-introduced royal face cards. The same happened in post-revolutionary Russia, where, until 1928, the royal images were illegal. Enough of this, let's have a look at some games from different cultures which children and young people enjoy playing!

TARROCCO

We thought that it would be fun to include one game which uses the full 78-card Tarot pack. It is one of the best known Tarot card games in Europe, but there are a number of local variations. In the version we've pieced together, Tarrocco is a three-player game. Because the game has passed through a number of cultures and countries, there are a number of unusual terms, but the game itself is not too difficult, and we feel that it is fun and different for young people to use the Tarot pack. They will be telling you your fortune next week!

A scorepad is needed both to note the scores and also to keep record of transactions, since players buy and sell cards during the game.

Major and Minor Arcana
The whole of the 22 cards in the Major Arcana are trumps. The highest value is XXI, the World down to the Juggler, value I, and the Fool, which has a value below I.

The Minor Arcana consists of the 56 cards divided into four suits of 14 cards: batons, cups, swords and coins. King ranks highest. The Juggler, the World and the Fool are called 'Honour' cards.

The object and the play

The dealer for the first hand is chosen by drawing a card, and convention has it that the lowest card gets to deal. Dealing and play takes place in an anti-clockwise direction. The player to the dealer's right is called the 'forehand', the second player, the 'middlehand' and the dealer the 'endhand.' If a player has 15 trumps in their hand they must declare them before play begins, and they earn ten bonus points.

The aim is to become the player with the highest score at the end of three hands. In Italy this is a gambling game and each loser pays up the difference in agreed money value between their points and the winner's score.

Each player is dealt 24 cards, one at a time, all face down. The dealer receives the extra six cards.

Once the cards have all been dealt out, players look at their hands and can begin to trade cards. This is an apparently 'optional' rule, but since it is unusual in UK card games, we would suggest that you at least try it. Players all suggest cards they would like to buy or trade. If it is a straight swop, no cost is involved, whereas a player buying a card pays ten points for a card they want. A record of these transactions is kept on the scoresheet. The skill lies in trying to build up suits, so that if a player wins a trick they can lead and continue to win further tricks. There is only one period of trading in the version we played.

The dealer discards six cards, then places one card as their lead, face up on the table. Play continues to the right. Each player must follow suit or trumps. It is like having five suits. If a player cannot follow suit they may play a trump or discard a card from another suit. Whoever wins the trick leads with a card for the next trick.

Two other peculiarities exist. **The Juggler:** If this is played in the last hand and wins, the player scores ten bonus points. Conversely, if the card is played in the last trick and loses, ten points are forfeited. **The Fool:** A player may display the fool instead of playing a card. When this occurs the other two players play out the trick, and the player with the fool card adds it to their own tricks.

Scoring

This is a bit of a pain! We believe that tricks all score five points per trick, but gain an additional bonus score if accompanied by a card from a suit in the lower arcana. The tricks which score bonus points include:

- The World, Juggler or Fool: extra five points for each
- Kings: four points each
- Queens: four points each
- Knights: two points each

A player who wins all of the tricks gains a bonus of 20 points.

The ultimate winner is the player with the highest score at the end of three hands.

Endnote: Because the rules and particularly the scoring are a bit odd, we strongly suggest that you try the games and then modify the rules and scoring to suit you and your participants.

A FEW CARD GAMES

We included a good number of card games suitable for young people in the *New Youth Games Book.* In this section we offer a few more which in their own way demonstrate that card playing spans the globe!

Slapjack

This may be American or British; it crops up in card game compilations of 'best card games for children' on both sides of the Atlantic. It's especially good for introducing young children to card games, since it's lively, noisy, and makes a change from 'Snap' and 'Pairs.'

You can play this with two or more players. Young players often beat their elders, so it can prove very popular with youthful participants. For two players use one pack of cards, for three or more, two packs mixed together are a good idea. You can even play this with a pack that is missing a few cards - very useful in many youth clubs and families!

Play begins with the cards all being dealt out one at time face down in piles in front of each of the players. Players mustn't look at their cards.

- The aim is to win all the cards, or win the most cards at the end of an agreed time period.
- The first player picks up the card from the top of their pile and turns it over and drops it in the middle of the table all in one swift movement. This is to ensure that the player does not see the card before it lands on the table.
- Each player goes through the same routine, until a jack is turned up. All the players then try to slap the jack, which means getting their palm on top of the jack on the table. The player whose hand is first onto the jack wins all the cards in the centre of the table.
- After a jack is won, all the cards are placed face down at the bottom of the winner's pile.
- If a player makes a false 'slap' they must give their top card to the person who dropped the card on the table.
- If a player runs out of cards they are allowed one more attempt to slapjack, before they must retire.

The game should be played fast. It can be a bit hard on table tops and adult nerves, but most children love it!

Le Vieux Garcon
This is a simple French game which is quite similar to 'Old Maid' in the UK and 'Black Peter' in Germany. Apparently all these type of games are based on a 16th century Italian gambling game called, 'Andare a Piscere.' You need three or more players, and it is particularly popular with young children. It is played with a standard pack, with the jacks of hearts, diamonds and clubs removed.

Play begins with all the cards being dealt out to the players. They then sort them out into pairs, three of a kind, two pairs and singles.
- Players can now put down on the table any pairs that they have, but not three of a kind.
- Taking turns, players fan out their cards, backs facing outwards. Their hand may include the jack of spades, known as the 'old boy.' The next player takes one of these cards and then tries make a new pair. And then it is their turn to fan their hand and allow the next player to choose a card.
- Gradually the jack is harder to get rid of as more and more pairs are placed on the table.
- There is no winner. Players retire when they have got rid of all their cards. The loser is the person left at the end with 'le vieux garcon.'

Happy Families
This can be played using special sets of cards or using a normal pack. Again, it is a universal game which seems to exist in most European countries. To play you need at least three players. The aim is to collect the most sets of families (four cards to a family).

In the special sets, cards are usually depicted as the four family members such as Mr Bun, the baker, Mrs Bun, Master Bun, Mistress Bun. The sets depicted below have four cards for the members of each family, or four of each nursery rhyme character. If you are using an ordinary set of cards, 'families' are the four cards of the same value: kings, tens, fives, aces or whatever.

Play
- The entire pack is dealt out, one card at a time.
- All the players sort out their hands so that they can see which families they have members of.
- The player to the dealer's left starts by asking one of the other players for either, (depending on the cards you are using), a particular member of a family or any card from that family. If they get a card, it continues to be their turn and they can request another card. Players may only ask for a card when they have at least one member of that family in their hand.
- When a player fails to get a card, their turn ends and the person they asked then attempts to win a card.
- When a player has all four members of a family they place these face down on the table.
- Play continues until all the families are assembled on the table. The player who has won the most families is the winner.

Go Boom

We've included this for two simple reasons: it is fun and we like the name of the game! It can be played by two or more players. It is quite simple to learn and can be played with or without using a scoring system. The aim is to be the first player to get rid of all the cards in their hand, which is called to 'Go Boom!'

Play begins with each player being dealt seven cards, face down. The remainder of the cards are place face down as a stockpile in the centre of the table.
- The first player places one card down on the table face up.
- The next player must try to follow with either a card of the same value or a card of the same suit. For instance after a 5♣ they can play any other 5, or any ♣.
- If they cannot play, they must pick up cards from the stockpile, one at a time until they can go.
- If there are no cards left in the stockpile the player who cannot go must 'pass.'
- On each round the cards are compared and the highest value card (aces high) wins. If the cards are all of the same value, the first card played wins the trick.

- When the last card is played, the player cries 'Go Boom' at which point they win that game.
- If the game is scored, the winner receives the value of all the cards left in their opponents' hands, based on a scoring system:
    - one point for an ace
    - ten points for a king, queen or jack
    - numeric value of any other card.

With young people, the winner is usually the first person to score 100 points. In family or adult groups, 200 is a more reasonable target. It is a good game for introducing younger children to the suits and the idea of winning tricks.

HAND GAMES
Hei Tama tu Tama

In Maori culture in New Zealand, hand games have been passed down through successive generations, partly as a form of amusement, but also as a means of teaching their children the quick eye and fast reactions of the warrior!

'Hei Tama tu Tama' is rather similar to 'Mora,' also known as 'Paper, Pencil, Scissors' (described in the *New Youth Games Book).* It is also an obvious relative of the British hand games of 'Tippet' and 'Up Jenkins' which we describe after the Maori game. No equipment whatsoever is required for 'Hei Tama tu Tama.' It is usually played by two players facing each other, but we also used it at a 'New Games' festival with a massive number of young people facing each other in two long lines.

Play begins with one player facing the other, with their hands on their hips, and challenging them, saying:

"*Hei Tama tu Tama*" and the other responds with "*Ae!*" *(meaning "Yes.")*
Then the challenger calls *Heiiiiiiiiiiiii Tama tu Tama*" again and on the second "*Tama*" both players immediately assume one of three different positions:

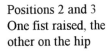

Starting position
Hands on hips

Position 1
Arms raised,
fists clenched

Positions 2 and 3
One fist raised, the
other on the hip

If the second player has matched the challenger's position they win a point and become the challenger. If the challenger wins, they gain a point and once more call, "*Hei Tama tu Tama*." The first person to win ten points is usually the winner.

Having seen the Tongan and Samoan rugby teams going through their pre-match taunts to the opposition, Alan is thinking of inviting his running club to adopt this chant as the ritual invitation to challengers at races!

Tippet or Up Jenkins

From the smoky world of pubs comes 'Tippet' and its slightly more complex cousin, 'Up Jenkins.' These have been well described by Arthur Taylor in both of his books on Pub Games. (Guinness Book of Traditional Pub Games. 1992) They are fast, simple and in pubs are usually gambling games, but they are equally fun for young people playing for points.

They are played by two teams of three players, and only one small coin is needed to play. Each team has a captain and they toss to decide who goes first. The winning captain then passes the coin from hand to hand between the three players in their team. This usually takes place underneath the table at which they are sitting, but can go on behind the backs of the team players. To keep the element of bluffing and chaos alive it is best if the players continue to talk and generally fool around.

♦ When the captain of the guessing team calls *"Hands up"* all six fists are placed on the table. The guessing team captain can now try to eliminate some of the hands by pointing to two, which are then exposed, however, if they **do** hold the coin the round ends with one point going to the team with the coin.
♦ Next, the captain may ask the team with the coin to *"Tighten them,"* which means that all the players must put their fists back under the table and increase their grip. The hand with the coin is likely to show signs of white round the knuckles.
♦ Finally, the captain puts his own hand palm upwards opposite the hand he thinks holds the coin. If it is a correct guess, the team gets the coin and takes its turn to hide it. If the guess is incorrect, the team with coin gains a point and again hides the coin.
♦ Only the team with the coin can score points. A game usually finishes at eleven points.

Up Jenkins

This is an extension of 'Tippet' and it allows the guessing team a couple of extra strategies for finding the coin.
1. The captain can ask for 'Smash 'ems,' which means that all the fists must be banged on the table.
2. The call of 'Crabs' means that all the fists must be raised with only fingertips touching the table. Thumbs are kept hidden, with one keeping the coin in its safe hiding place.
3. On 'Church windows' all the fists are held up for inspection with fingers splayed out, palms inwards and the thumb once again holding the coin (or nothing).
If the coin is dropped at any time, which is quite likely, the coin passes immediately to the opposing team.

With groups of young people it is best to start with 'Tippet' and then progress to 'Up Jenkins.'

NUMBER PAIRS

This is a simple but quite interesting and entertaining paper and pencil competition for two players. To start with, a piece of paper is prepared with the numbers 1 to 15 written on it, then a second set of 1 to 15 are added. Make sure that the second set are randomly placed across the sheet. It is usually best to put a ring round the numbers. Now, players take turns to join together pairs of numbers, starting with one, then two and so on. Play continues until one player cannot join their pair together without crossing another line. The person who cannot go is the loser. It sounds simple, but it almost always becomes tricky later on.

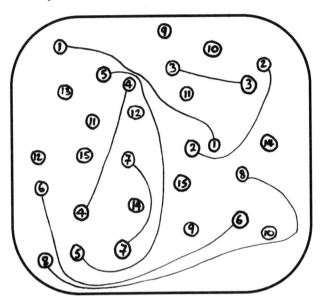

PACHISI

Pacis is the Hindi word for twenty-five, the highest score in Pachisi. The game is almost definitely an Indian invention, though it has spread in slightly modified forms throughout Sri Lanka, Burma, Syria, Iran, Somalia and Spain. In a rather different form, it was introduced into the UK in 1896 as 'Ludo' and 'Ludo Royale.' It is also quite similar to an Aztec and Mexican gambling game known as 'Patolli,' which was dedicated to Macuilxo-Chitl, the God of Sport and Gambling.

In India there are many variations on the rules of Pachisi. Hopefully, by talking to friends and comparing versions in other books, the version presented here is reasonably universal. When we encountered it first, we thought that it was not worth including, but when we played it, the use of small cowrie shells rather than dice and the tactical variations make it much more entertaining and stimulating than Ludo.

You can easily make a board, which can be as intricate or plain as you want to make it. The layout is as follows:

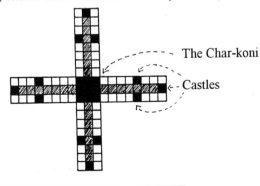

The Char-koni

- Castles

Play: In India, each player has four wooden pieces shaped a little like an acorn with a flattened base. Their tops are painted with distinctive patterns. With young people we tried to always have four players since it makes the game more exciting than with two or three.

As well as the board and sixteen playing pieces, six cowrie shells are required. These have a rounded back and an open top. In Pachisi, unlike Ludo, all the playing pieces start in the central reservation, called Char-koni. Each playing piece enters the game down the player's central trackway and then proceeds for a full circuit, moving anti-clockwise around the outside track, finally to re-enter on the same middle track, when they are then placed on their sides to indicate that they have been completely round the board.

However, this is where Pachisi starts to vary from the more simple game of Ludo!

To move their pieces, players throw the six cowrie shells and how they land determines the number of squares they can move one of their pieces.
- two cowries with tops open....2 squares
- three cowries with tops open...3 squares
- four cowries with tops open...4 squares
- five cowries with tops open...5 squares
- six cowries with tops open...6 squares and another go
- one cowrie with top open...10 squares and another go
- no cowries with top open...25 squares and another go (Pachisi)

On the first turn for each player, they can move out a piece from the Char-koni whatever they throw, but subsequently other pieces can only move out when a 6, 10 or 25 is thrown. To get a piece back safely to the Char-koni, the exact number must be thrown, and then the piece is removed from the board. A player may decide not to take a throw, or not to move a piece, otherwise the whole value of the throw must be used for the movement of a single piece.

Places of Safety, Capturing and Doubling-up:
All the dark squares on the board represent castles, which are places of safety. If a piece lands on a castle square, that piece is safe from capture by the enemy, but a player's own pieces or those of their partner (in a double's game) may share the castle. As in Ludo, any player's piece which lands on an already occupied square can capture an opponent's piece and knock it back to the Char-koni. When a piece lands on a square already occupied by another of the same player's pieces, they can be doubled-up. In practice this means that they can only be captured by a piece of the same or greater strength; they can now move together with each throw, and they form a blockade which prevents any other pieces, including the player's own, from overtaking them.

It is an inherently unfriendly, tactical game, and some younger children may fall out with each other if their pieces keep re-visiting the Char-koni. You've been warned!

THE GAME OF BOOKS
We had been playing games of comprehension and bluff based on books long before the Bodleian Library joined forces with Oxford Games to market some of them in attractive packages with names such as 'Ex Libris' and 'Bookworm'. We think both these games are good, but you can easily improvise and make up your own versions.

We have used both of the commercial games with adolescent groups and adults, and Bookworm, which is simpler, has a nicely illustrated board and is suitable for reasonably well-motivated ten year olds. Our game, like those from Oxford, does require reading skills from either all the players, or at least from one member of each team. We have used it with groups of mixed ages, minimum age about eleven.

To prepare for the playing of our game you need to do a little bit of illicit photocopying on the work photocopier.

- Photocopy about forty random pages from a variety of different books. Try to choose books appropriate to the reading age of your games players.
- Then cut out a paragraph from each, trying to select sections which end on a reasonably exciting bit.
- Stick these onto a blank A4 sheet of paper and write at the top of each the author, book title and a code number (one, two, three etc.).
- Now, write down four alternative versions of what happens next, including the correct one. (label them A, B, C and D.)
- Finally, make up an answer sheet, so you know the correct answers.

Your set of forty pages will be enough for up to four rounds, or games, of this sequence.

To play, you need a group of at least three participants, but really it works best in larger groups. Invite the players to take it in turns round the group to act as 'reader', reading aloud the paragraph and the four alternative versions of 'what happens next'. They will probably need to read out the A-D list a second time. Then, everyone writes down which letter they think is the most likely solution. The organiser (probably you) tells the group the correct answer and everyone with the right answer scores a point. About ten rounds is about enough to make the game fun and avoid boredom setting in.

A variation

Once players understand the basic game, it is possible to change the rules. In preparation for this version, the games facilitator must write down on a piece of paper the correct version of what comes next. They also need a stock of pieces of paper the same size. What happens is that following on from the reading of the paragraph out loud, everyone is invited to write down a short version of what happens next. These are gathered in together with the correct answer. If any of them are the same as the correct answer, one (or more)version is/are removed. The facilitator labels each ending with a letter or number; they are shuffled, and all read out. Then, everyone makes a guess at the solution.

Scoring:

- One point is awarded for each right guess.
- One point is given to the writer of each version which got a vote.
- After each round, each player's score is totalled up and written down by the game organiser.

DOTS AND LINES

We learned this variation on 'Sprouts,' described in the *New Youth Games Book,* from an American lady who was travelling though Scotland some years ago. It's a two-player game, the aim being to force your opponent to draw the last line. We played it on a five by five dot grid, but there really is no reason why you couldn't play it on smaller or bigger grids which are either squares or rectangles.

Firstly, draw up a five by five grid of dots. Then, start play with the first player joining up as many dots as they wish as long as they are in a single straight line. It is then the other player's turn. The same rule applies. In addition, it is permissible to:

- continue the line from either end of the existing line, but it must be continuous and not cross any other line, nor join to any other dot which already has a line touching or intersecting it.

The loser is the person who makes the last legal line.

In the following example, one player's line is unbroken, the other is dotted:

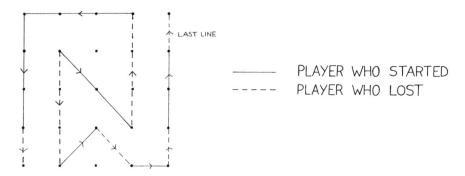

This is very easy to learn and can be played by young children as well as adolescents.

INVENTING A GAME: BERT'S GATE

This serves as an interesting example of how games - in this instance a diabolical board game - can be created spontaneously. The driving force behind the creation of 'Bert's Gate' was the wish to keep a semi-permanent record of the experiences of a small group of about 20 or so young people and adults, an assortment of tents, travellers' vehicles and a wonderful marquee - the purpose of which will be revealed over the following pages.

That this small group was part of a much larger group - somewhere between 100,000 and 120,000 people - may help explain why our experiences were interesting and why we wanted to record them in some kind of way. Packing that many people into several (very large!) fields guarantees that all human life will be there.

Into this mix insert the unique lushness and glory of the English countryside in summer; incredibly good, cheap food of any ethnic variety you care to think about; loads of wonderful market stalls - and you're probably well on the way to guessing where Big Al and Howie were for a few glorious days in summer '94.

The final ingredients in the mix are to position the whole lot - courtesy of an amazing human being called Michael Eavis - just a stone's throw from the magic of Stonehenge around the time of the summer Solstice; and to provide a superb variety of music, drama, theatre, comedy and other activities.

Yes, we're talking about Glastonbury 1994 - the penultimate one, as it may turn out to be, and about a band called Zion Train - except we've just remembered that we are writing a games book rather than a guide to Glastonbury! Still, many of you would *not* forgive us if we didn't tell you about Zion Train - they are *unbelievably* good, and the only band we've seen in recent years who create a highly political fusion of reggae, dub, jazz, club, rave & techno.

The Game - Setting and Terms

Bert is a guy who 'runs' one of the pedestrian gates at Glastonbury - tens of thousands of people pass through each of these gates daily (in both directions) over the festival period. The person in charge of each gate has typically been hand picked by Michael Eavis and has demonstrated their ability to control entry to and from the festival site in an honest, fair and humane manner over a number of years.

Bert has been running a gate for a decade at least and looks after home comforts for his team of people. Hence the marquee in which people can crash after their shifts - see, it all begins to make some kind of sense!

Security is different (completely!) from the teams that organise the gates. Security staff wear throat microphones and fluorescent jackets with 'SECURITY' on the back. They operate in small groups of half a dozen or so, and apart from regular patrols have the chilling ability to appear suddenly in large numbers at virtually any point in the site - on foot and in a variety of vehicles. They are fairly fair, but totally hard, and undoubtedly culled from special services of various kinds. Alan and Howie had a run-in with security..........but to find out what happened, you'll just have to play 'Bert's Gate!'

Main Stage - all the big name acts appear on this stage; The Levellers were powerful and brilliant that year (but Zion Train need more of a plug than they do!), Johnny Cash was interesting and Elvis Costello disappointing - people wanted to *boogie* but were doled out what sounded like MOR ('middle of the road').

MME Stage - indie bands and sounds.

Acoustic Stage - no explanation necessary we hope!

Jazz Stage - ditto, but it covers world music as well.

Sound Systems - dozens of the market traders who set up shops or cafes at the Fest turn their pitches into sound systems at night. They range from modest domestic stereos to mega systems which would do the most crazed Rasta person proud. So at 4 am, bleary eyed and pretty knackered, it's still possible for ageing hippies - or you - to stumble across dozens of insomniacs bopping away to smooth soul sounds or frenetic techno.

Green Fields - entertainment for children and families, together with all the alternative stuff. One of the nicest things we saw was a pedal-powered disco which needed three or four people peddling away like mad on bicycle type things to make a decent noise!

Lats - the only downside of Glastonbury is the latrines. Emptied every day, they still honk. Every year one or two people fall in. One year a 40 person lat collapsed ....

How the game works

We wanted to avoid having a game based solely on throwing a dice, so what we thought up is as follows:

Make up a set of 60 cards, each of equal size. On twenty of the cards is a distinctive event from the life of the Glastonbury Festival. The other forty cards have an instruction on to move either:

   -Looking for some action, move 3 spaces (five cards)
   -Need some supplies, move 2 spaces (ten cards)
   -Move on to the next place; 1 space (ten cards)
   -Chill out and stay where you are (five cards)

A game lasts three complete rounds of the cards. On each turn a player takes one card and follows the instruction, moving their playing piece round the board. The card is then placed face up on the discard pile. When all the cards are on the discard pile they are shuffled and placed face down for the next round of the game. On each of the sites marked '**?**' there are four experience tokens, which can be collected by landing on the special squares. The aim is to collect the most 'Glastonbury Experiences' by the end of the game.

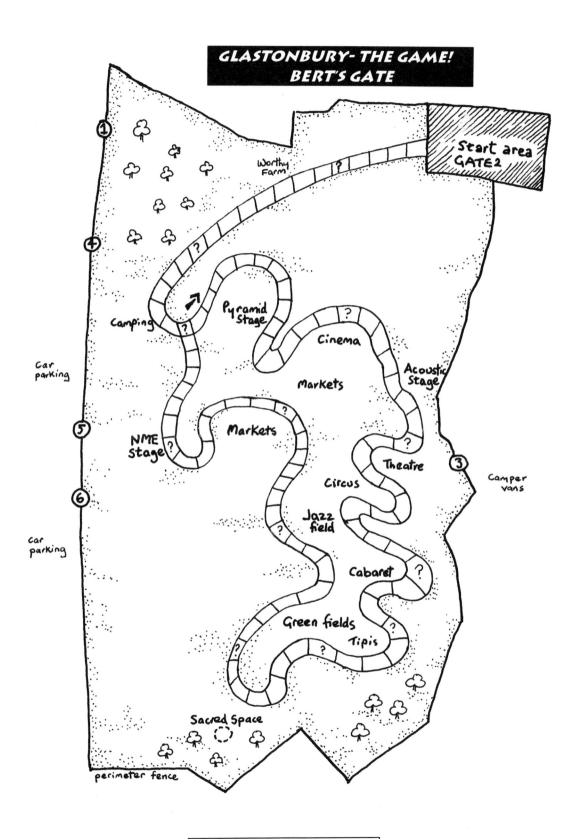

GLASTONBURY- THE GAME!
BERT'S GATE

Start area
GATE 2

Worthy
Farm

Camping

Pyramid
Stage

Cinema

Markets

Acoustic
Stage

Car
parking

NME
Stage

Markets

Theatre

Circus

Camper
vans

Jazz
field

Cabaret

Green fields

Tipis

car
parking

Sacred Space

perimeter fence

The reason for including this game is not so much to get you to play it, rather it is an invitation to you and your friends to invent a game of your own!

Ideas for special cards:

Listen to Billy Nasty performing his '3D UFO' set in one of the market areas. Exhilarated. Move 3 spaces.

Finally find the Cabaret tent and enjoy a live performance of Juke Box Jury with the audience as the jury. Don't want the show to end after trashing Cliff Richard's Summer Holiday record. Stay put and miss a turn.

Caught in the circus field in a sudden downpour of rain. Stuck in the mud and miss a turn.

Get chased by a deranged streaker. Go back two spaces.

Customs and Excise officials search you 'on suspicion' that you are selling imported tobacco. Miss a turn.

Caught up in an armed robbery at one of the beer tents - extricate yourself from these nasty security people and go back 3 spaces

Your tent's been nicked - find a friendly neighbour with a spare sleeping bag and miss a turn

40,000 are exiting NME Stage after The Orbital gig and you lose your friends in the crowd - go back 2 spaces

After the Zion Train gig you find yourself without a carry-out and buy a Tequila Slammer from a (closed!) bar. The bar person hasn't seen anyone down a slammer in one for a long time and gives you a bottle of wine - carry-out problem solved. Move one space and draw an extra card

Have a brilliant time at the Zion Train gig - undoubtedly the best new band this side of the new millennium - move on three spaces

Score a bulk distribution deal for the 'Time to Travel' book you are selling at the festival - move on three spaces

Blag a Hospitality Pass from Main Stage security person. Costs you one copy of 'Time to Travel' but worth it as you can cruise in and out of the Press Tent in search of the one and only 'Peely'. You find him subtly disguised in a parka and lager lout sun hat. He is gracious, charming and accepts a copy of Time to Travel. Mission accomplished - move on one space and take an extra turn.

Bump into Sid Rawle - 'King of the Hippies' - who insists on telling you his exploits since the glory days of 1968 - time consuming so miss a turn.

Bop to the sound system of 'The Serious Road Trip' and have extensive and deep discussions about their work in running aid into the toughest war zones. You decide to volunteer immediately for the next Serious Road Trip to Bosnia. The real game of life begins - leave the site and the game immediately via pedestrian gate 3.

UNIVERSITY LIBRARY

You leave the site by gate 2 to get your reserve supply of Irn Bru and munchies. Lady Luck fails you resulting in a mugging during which you lose your cash - and more importantly your pass back into the site. Lose a turn.

Tim (another Gate Controller) spots you wearing a Hospitality pass and does a berserker, accusing you of being the perpetrator of stealing a box of them earlier in the day. You eventually calm him down. Move back two spaces.

A security team spots you sitting by the roadside selling copies of the 'Time to Travel' book - apparently you need a pass to do this. Security refuse to believe Alan's explanation that Michael Eavis invited him on site to sell the books. Miss a turn while Alan goes off in search of a pass.

At 3 a.m. you happen on a sound system playing the coolest soul sounds you've heard in a long while. The DJ is so good he must surely do this professionally. Greatly invigorated so move on 3 spaces.

Your so-called best buddy has pitched the tent right next to the hi-tech Hare Krishna marquee (Hare Krishna chants accompanied by electric guitar and electronic keyboards). Like, man, they *never* stop chanting ...... Hare Krishna - Hare Krishna - Hare Hare etc. This is bad karma indeed. Go in search of serious ear plugs and miss a turn.

No cash and ravenous - no alternative to eating humble pie and mega fart inducing macrobiotic scran in the Krishna tent. Oh no! They've got you - go back 3 spaces

SPELLICANS

Sometimes called 'Spillikins' this game can be played by anywhere between two and six players. It originates from China and is the original source for the game of 'Pick up sticks' or 'Jackstraws.' It may be hard to find a set, but they have been manufactured in plastic in the UK and it is a more interesting game than Pick up sticks.

A full set of spellicans consists of between 60 and 100 intricately carved/shaped sticks, which each have a points value, depending upon how hard they are to pick up. Each set also includes a special hook piece, which players use in turn to try and pick up a piece from the pile.

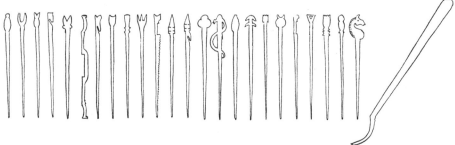

Play begins with one player holding all the spellicans together in a bundle and letting them fall (without any interference) onto the floor or table. We found it best to play on a carpet. On each turn, players attempt to remove a single spellican with the hook. They must accomplish this without moving any other piece. If a player is successful, they add the spellican to their pile and try to lift out another spellican. When they fail, play moves on to the next player. Once a player has touched a particular piece, they *must continue to try to lift that piece.* At the end of the game the value of all the pieces each player has hooked is added up. Some of the pieces are very hard to lift out because of their serrated edges. The 'saw' shaped piece scores fifty points.

If you do find a set, they are cheap, quite popular with young people, even to play on their own, and it doesn't ruin the game if a piece or two get broken or go 'missing! Original sets were made of bone, or ivory (which we won't use on principle). They are quite collectable if in good condition.

CAROMS

Sometimes spelled 'Carums' or 'Carroms' depending where your set originated. To play this game you have to fork out money for a board and a set of disks (called caroms). Alan first discovered a board in the activity room of Bray's Grove Youth Centre in Harlow, Essex, but didn't know what it was and therefore was never able to play it. That was in 1972. Since then, Alan has been appropriately embarrassed by local carom-players in a beach shack in Goa, and had his friend Himu Gupta from Norwich extol its virtues:

> "*It's a wonderful game, which probably developed through the activities of the British East India Company from around 1650. It is a combination of British talent and Bengali native ingenuity.*"

In a book of 'youth' games, we can wholeheartedly recommend carom as a useful addition to the equipment cupboard at a youth club, or as a very good family game for the home. It's not cheap, costing in the UK between £45 and £100 for a reasonable board. Boards are available from a number of good games shops including 'Just Games' at 71 Brewer Street in London and Hamley's toystore. The smoothness of the board defines the quality of the board, since the caroms must slide across the wooden surface.

Originally the game was played in India, Burma and the Yemen. The size of boards vary, but the most common has a playing surface of two foot square, with solid sides to provide the equivalent of the cushions in pool and snooker, and four small netted pockets in the corners. Friction on the table is reduced by applying French chalk. We would describe it as a creative mixture of shove ha'penny, billiards and marbles.

The aim of the game for each player is to:
- knock in all their nine (black or white) caroms with the striker disk;
- pocket the red queen disk, provided that the same player pockets another of their own caroms immediately afterwards;
- leave the opponent with as many caroms as possible left on the board.

The board and the starting position of the carom game is:

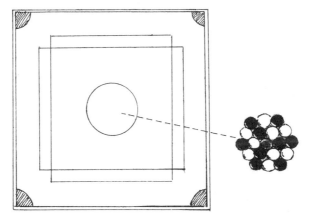

Rules for the game vary slightly in different localities, but we believe that the set we offer here are fairly universal. We learned the hard way, since the original rules we obtained with our set were very loosely translated from the original Hindi!

The game is played by either two players, or two teams of two players, who sit with their partners opposite. Usually, the decision on who goes first is made by one player hiding a black carom in one closed fist. If the other player chooses this fist, they go first, aiming to pot the black caroms. The first player puts the striker disk anywhere in the rectangle in front of them, and flicks the striker in a forward direction aiming at the white carom pieces. We were taught that any finger or the thumb can be used to flick the striker, with the aim of hitting one of the their own caroms into a pocket. This can be accomplished through a straight hit, rebounding off the sides into a carom, or by ricocheting into one or more caroms. If the player pockets a white carom, they get another go, returning the striker to the shooting rectangle. That player continues until they fail to pot one of their caroms, or they commit a foul shot. Then, the other player has their turn, shooting at the black caroms.

Foul shots:
- If a player pots one of their opponent's caroms, their turn ends and the carom stays in the pocket, or is pulled out of the pocket and placed on the wooden side.

- If a player knocks a carom off the board, it is replaced back on the board as near as possible to the centre spot, and that turn ends.
- If the striker is pocketed, the turn ends, and the opponent can place one of the previously potted pieces back anywhere in the centre of the board.
- If the striker and a carom are pocketed in the same shot, the opponent replaces the potted carom anywhere in the centre, and takes the striker for their own turn.
- If the queen is pocketed but this is not followed by another of that player's caroms, the queen is put back in the middle, and any other caroms potted during that turn.

The potting of the queen is only successful if that player pots another of their caroms in their next strike.

Two alternatives to this rule apply in some regions:
One: The queen can only be potted after the player has potted one carom, and before they pot a further carom.
Two: The queen can only be potted as the last shot, immediately after the player has potted their own nine caroms.

Scoring:
- No scoring takes place until one player has pocketed all their caroms.
- The player who has pocketed all the caroms then scores one point for each of their opponent's caroms still left on the table.
- The queen scores five points to the person who has cleared their caroms, if they pocketed it successfully during the 'board' (one round of the full game).
- The queen's value falls to four points after a player has reached 24 points in the full game.
- If the striker is potted before a player has scored in a 'board', that player receives a minus-one penalty point.
- A 'set' is won when one player reaches 30 points after a number of 'boards' have been played. (In match play, the winner is the person who first wins two out of three 'sets'.)

SQUAILS

This is basically a table version of bowls. As far as we know there is no commercially available set of squails now made, but it is very easy to improvise. In R.C.Bell's book, *Board and Table Games from Many Civilizations (Dover)* he entertainingly quotes from an English emigrant's diary, while he was bound for Australia on the clipper ship, the Orient:

> *"our amusements grow stale and insipid; though the never failing cards, chess, backgammon, and draughts serve to while away the weary hours. Squails, in which the ladies join and are becoming dangerous rivals for the gentlemen, have a large patronage."*

Since many homes and youth clubs have quite large, round tables which is the major requirement, this game can easily be used in a wide range of places where there are young people.

To play you need four round disks marked in a distinctive colour for each player. These can be draughts or round gaming counters or even small drink coasters. You also need one heavy metal disk; we used a fifty pence piece when using draughts as squails. We have played squails with anything between two and eight players; about four seems

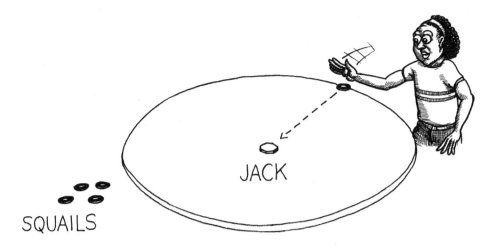

JACK

SQUAILS

ideal. Players can play as individuals or can play in teams of pairs.

- To start, the metal 'jack' is placed in the centre of the table as a target.
- Players then take it in turns to push or shove one of their squails, with the aim of getting it as close as possible to the jack. They accomplish the push in the same way as in shove ha'penny, by placing the squail partly over the edge of the table and then striking it with the palm of the hand.
- They are allowed to bump into opponent's squails and also to try and nudge their own squails closer to the jack.
- If the jack is moved more than six inches away from centre of the table it is replaced in the centre.
- Squails which end up off the table or within three inches of the edge of the table are considered dead.
- Knocking the jack off the table carries a two point penalty.
- When all the squails have been played, scoring is carried out. The squail furthest away from the jack scores one point, next closer gets two points and so on.

Games consist of an agreed number of rounds.

One tip: have a tape measure handy to prevent heated arguments breaking out!

PLANKS

This game seems to have been played widely in the United States just before the beginning of the twentieth century. It is an interesting variation on noughts and crosses, called tic-tac-toe in the States, and can be played by two, three or four players.

We found it easy enough for young people to learn but it does require the preparation of twelve special **'planks.'** We made ours from thin plywood, using a fretsaw and then painting the wood with acrylic multi-surface pens, but you can easily make a playable set out of reasonably solid cardboard. The twelve planks are made to measure about 3 x 1 centimetres. You need to make four of each of the following colour variations:

RED WHITE BLUE   RED BLUE WHITE   BLUE RED WHITE

You also need 24 small **counters,** divided into four sets of six counters, marked A, B, C and D. We bought some cheap gaming counters and marked them with the letters using a permanent black marker. In each set, two counters must be red, two blue and two white.

The start of the game determines which set of counters each player is to use. With two players, mix up an A and a B counter face-down. Each player chooses a letter-counter, then picks up the rest of their letter set. With three players use A, B and C. With four players, use all four letters, with players operating as two teams: A and C sit opposite one another and play against B and D.

Regardless of the number of players, the planks are shuffled face down, then,
- with two players, each player chooses six planks;
- with three players, each player chooses four planks;
- with four players, each player chooses three planks;
In each case, the players put their planks face up in front of them on the table, so they are visible to the other player(s).

The aim of the game is the same as in noughts and crosses, namely to make a line of three counters (three As/Bs/Cs or Ds). They must include one blue, one red and one white counter, but in any order. A line must be horizontal or vertical, but not diagonal. You'll get the idea as we explain the method of play. Really!

On each turn, a player may **either** place down a plank *and* put one counter of the appropriate colour on top of it, **OR** put one counter on to a matching coloured square of another plank already on the table. Planks are always placed with long sides touching one another, as in the diagram below.

When all of a player's counters have been played, they must move one counter already placed on the planks to a new position (but still of matching colour). Once a player's planks have all been played the only option is to move a counter to a new position in order to construct a line.

The game is one of clever strategy and the colours add an important new dimension to the noughts and crosses game. We found it was popular with a variety of young people from the age of about eight upwards.

Where there are four players, each may only play their own individual planks and counters. A team wins when either player completes a winning line.

DICTIONARY GAME

We have always tried to introduce young people to games using words. Words have helped us to earn a living and it seems likely that skill with words will continue to be a marketable commodity for a long time to come.

The Dictionary game has been marketed as 'Balderdash' by two enterprising Canadians, but you can play it for free! It is a very funny game for about four or more players and mixes bluffing and guessing. All you need to play is a dictionary (the bigger the better) and a stock of paper and pens/pencils. Penguin have even published a special 'Dictionary Game Dictionary' compiled by James Cochrane, which only has unusual and obscure words in it. It is best played only by people who know how to use a dictionary and do not find it threatening, though we have used it with nine and ten year olds, for whom it provides a fun way of actually making use of the dictionary.

There are a number of sets of rules for this game, but the way we have successfully played it with groups is as follows:
- cut up pieces of paper that are all of similar sizes, say about three inches wide by one inch deep;
- make sure that players cannot see what each other is writing;
- one player chooses an unusual word (usually using the dictionary as a resource), unlikely to be known by anyone in the group; they then read and spell this out aloud;
- if anyone knows the meaning of the word, another word is chosen;
- all the players including the dictionary 'holder' write down a short definition each on their slips of paper; if there are only three or four players, the holder can add in an extra invented definition;
- all the slips of paper are handed in and shuffled round then read quickly by the holder to weed out any nearly correct definitions. All of the definitions are now read out aloud including the correct one and then the game can be scored, or not as the group decides.

The game is essentially non-competitive, but if you want to score it one way is as follows: Players who vote for the correct definition gain one point as do players who wrote almost correct definitions by chance. Players whose deviant definitions get chosen as 'correct' by other players get two points for each vote they gain. If no player recognises the correct definition, the holder gets two points.

As players get used to the game they will realise that the skill is in deceiving each other with realistic, believable -sounding definitions. It is also the source of most of the fun! To start you off and give you a feeling for the game, what is the correct definition of:

curmurmering

Is it?
1. A type of tobogganing used in Sweden.
2. A fart or loud rumbling noise.
3. A dressmaking term for hemming on a curved last.
4. The sound made by the Elizabethan curmur instrument.
5. A form of street pickpocketing using a small team of thieves.
Answer at the bottom of the page.

MANCALA GAMES

We were rather afraid of including any mancala games in our original *Youth Games Book* simply because there were so many of them! These are amongst the most universally played games in the world, and whilst there are literally hundreds of variations, the basic style of play is similar in them all. The name mancala seems to have come from the arabic word 'manqala', meaning to move. Most people in the UK have probably seen the boards, which are usually made from a solid block of wood, hollowed out into a series of bowls, which vary in number between three and 108 cups. The earliest boards are believed to be about 3,500 years old and have been found in ancient remains around Egypt and Luxor.

Nowadays, the game is extensively played in most states of Africa, Southern India and Ceylon. It is also a common street game in the Caribbean. Most of the time, the mancala games are played by children or men. In typically sexist fashion, when women in many of the African countries have shown themselves to be good at the game, they are then *not* allowed to play! Having looked at a number of the games, we decided to explain the rules of just one, since you must always ask people *exactly* how they play mancala since it is inevitably a little bit different each time.

Another aspect of mancala which is interesting is the significance attached in many cultures to the boards themselves. The making of a mancala board is viewed as hazardous, and in some places only men whose wives have died are willing to risk making a new board. They are usually roughly hewn, since the smoothing of them is meant to be a part of the ritual of playing the game. You can either make a board, improvise one on a sheet of card, or buy one from a specialist games shop. You probably will not be frightened by the legend which prevents many African tribesmen from playing the game after dark - they fear that ghosts or spirits will come and join in the game!

Awari

This is also known as Wari and Owari, and is a very common game in West Africa. The game uses twelve cups, six for each of the two players, with one scoring cup at each end.

Number two

The playing pieces are small stones, seeds or beans; 48 are needed for Awari. In the UK, boards are sometimes supplied with marbles. The aim of the game is to capture more pieces than the opponent.

Play begins by placing four beans in each of the 12 cups. The six bowls closest to each player is their 'side.'

- Players take it in turns to 'sow' their seeds, which means taking all the pieces from any one bowl and placing one each in the adjacent bowls in a clockwise direction.

- If a bowl contains twelve or more pieces, the sowing will cover more than one complete circuit of the board. In this case, no piece is sown into the bowl from which the pieces have been lifted.
- A player captures pieces from their opponent when they can sow seeds into bowls on the opposite side of the board which make the contents total 2 or 3. They then move all the pieces from those bowls into their scoring bowl. However, a player may not capture all their opponents' pieces and must leave one bowl, of their choice, intact.
- When a player is left with no pieces in any of their cups, the opponent must attempt to sow seeds into the opposition side.
- The game ends when one player is unable to play.
- The winner is the player with the highest number of pieces captured.

Because the logic of the game is somewhat unusual, it is rather easier to play than to explain! Children and young people we have introduced the game to seem to enjoy it, but you must play a few rounds with them first to get them used to the method of play.

SCRABBLE VARIATIONS

We waxed lyrical about 'Scrabble' in our 'New Youth Games Book,' but we only included one variation you could play using the standard set of tiles and board. In that book we mentioned some of the Scrabble derivative games such as Scrabble Dice and Scrabble Rebus. Here we would like to say a few words about where Scrabble comes from, how it is used in different countries with different languages, and offer a few games variations which may add a little zest to any Scrabble playing you organise.

Scrabble became a huge craze in the 1950s, soon after it was invented by Alfred M. Butts in America. There are always 100 tiles in a set, but depending on which country you are playing the game in, the distribution of letters varies. For instance, there are 15 Es in the French set (12 in the UK) and in the Netherlands they use 10 Ns (6 here) and two Js (instead of our one). The idea of multi-lingual Scrabble may sound appealing, but it just will not work because of the different use of letters in each language. We have an original set which has beautiful wooden tiles made in Germany; nowadays the tiles are made of plastic. Our last piece of nearly 'useless' information is that in America getting all seven letters out in one go is called a 'Bingo.'

Five start variation

Frequently, Scrabble starts off slowly because very short words are played at the start. In this variation, the person who has won the right to go first does so **only** if they can put down a word of at least five letters. If they cannot go, the right to start moves to the next player, and so on. If no-one can start with a five letter word or longer, the same process is repeated with the aim of starting with a four letter word, then three letters and so on.

Bonus point Scrabble
Before starting this game variation, players agree to a category of word having a bonus value of 25 points. For instance, types of animal, colours, vehicles, or foods could be chosen.

Double bag Scrabble
One of the aspects of Scrabble which puts off many young people or beginners are the occasional dreadful combinations of tiles which may be drawn from the bag. We have both experienced horrific collections such as: A,A,I,E,E,U,Z! Butts and his marketing colleague, James Brunot, offer a solution to this frustration. Before beginning play, separate out the 42 vowels and the 56 consonants into two separate bags, adding one blank into each bag. Then, throughout the game, players can draw the letters they need, choosing all from one bag or some from each. It does help stop any players getting too fed up!

Recycler Scrabble
In this version of the game, each time the blank is played, the following player(s) has the opportunity to exchange the correct letter for the blank, as well as having their normal turn. They do not have to re-use the blank on that turn, but they may not exchange the blank on a turn when they are passing. Eventually, the blanks are 'frozen' when all the real tile versions of the letter represented by the blank are on the board. With this recycling of the blank, scores are significantly increased, and it adds a further competitive dimension to the game.

Solo Scrabble
We have on a number of occasions been asked whether there is a solo version of Scrabble. Here it is! This is useful for people living alone, the bed-ridden or even for travellers, who can use the Travel Scrabble pack.

What happens is that a single player sets up two racks, then times themself against the clock, playing each hand in turn. It is hard to suggest a definite time limit for players of varying abilities, but somewhere in the 30-60 minutes range seems about right. This allows a few minutes for scoring. After playing Solo Scrabble a few times, a player will be able to judge how well (or badly) they are playing! The combined score for two players is likely to be between 300 and 400. The world record for an individual player's score is held by an Australian and is 725 points. For most players, scoring more than 300 in a game is cause for celebration.

JEWISH PASSOVER: FESTIVAL OF FREEDOM
We have worked for a couple of Jewish organisations in our youth working lives, and whilst not ourselves Jewish, we have gained much from our contact with some Jewish youngsters and adults who have subsequently become very good friends. David Jacobs, from the Reform Synagogues of Britain, who is a particular friend, responded to my request for Jewish games, by saying that he couldn't think of anything in particular. His actual reply was:
>"We take your games from the 'New Youth Games Book' and Jewify them!"

We decided this was a challenge and so looked out for something we *could* include. In an American book called 'A pumpkin in a pear tree' (Ann Cole et al. Little Brown. 1974.) we found some interesting information about making the Pesach, Passover celebration, more relevant to young people. The celebration marks the exodus of the Jews from Egypt and is known as the Festival of Freedom. The Seder is the special meal that Jewish families celebrate and each item on the menu has special significance. For Jewish families, the Seder meal takes place on Seder night, when the Passover Hagadah book is read aloud. We experimented by holding a Passover meal with a group of children, none of them Jewish, in March last year. They all knew a bit about the Exodus from school religious lessons, but seemed to really enjoy participating in the activity of making the Seder meal and learning about some of its special meanings.

The meal celebrates the approach of Spring as well as the Exodus. The Seder plate has on it:

- ❏ Roasted meat on the bone, which symbolises the *paschal,* the sacrificial offering.
- ❏ A hard-boiled egg, symbolic of Spring and the survival of the children of Israel.
- ❏ A small bowl of salt water to dip the food in, as a remembrance of the tears of slavery and the escape from that slavery.
- ❏ Matzos, which are unleavened bread, reminiscent of the bread baked by the Jewish people during their exile in the desert.
- ❏ Haroseth, which is a dip or spread for the matzos, and represents the bricks and mortar that the Hebrews used to build the monuments for the Pharaohs in Egypt.
- ❏ Horseradish sauce, represents the bitter herbs - the bitterness of slavery.

At the traditional family dinner, an extra glass of wine is left on the table, and the door to the room is left open for Elijah to bring news of freedom. Some of our Caribbean friends make similar meals which have a symbolic significance representing a return to Africa from the far flung nations where they now reside.

The recipes for the unusual elements of this meal are:

Matzos
Mix three and half times as much flour, by volume, with water. You may add a little salt. Mix the dough and knead it. Roll out the dough quite thinly. and place it on a greased

baking tray and cut into squares. Prick the dough all over with a fork. Bake in a pre-heated oven at 475 degrees centigrade for 10 to 15 minutes or when lightly brown on top.

Haroseth

As already mentioned, this makes a good dip or spread for the matzos. Add together, one cup of chopped apple with a quarter of a cup of finely chopped nuts, one teaspoon of cinnamon and two table spoons of grape juice or wine. We crunched this all together until it was a thickish spread with a few lumpy bits; it tasted nice!

And to the end: the Afikomon

Apparently the Seder cannot finish until there is a hunt for the 'Afikomon' which is the middlemost matzo. Traditionally the father at the meal wraps this matzo in a serviette and hides it somewhere in an agreed area of the building. The children then search it out as the 'treasure.' When it is found, the father gives it back to all the members of the 'family,' who must all sample it to bring the Seder to a fitting communal conclusion.

This whole celebration can easily be adapted to a group situation, and is an interesting introduction to the Jewish culture.

CURVED BALL

This puzzle has turned up in a number of puzzle compendiums both in the USA and the UK. To use it, make a photocopy of the larger shapes on this page, preferably on card, and without the answer at the bottom of the page! Cut out the shapes, and ask your player(s) to try and construct a perfect circle. Because all the curves follow the same radius, it is a nasty little puzzle to solve, even though it seems easy at first! Good Luck!

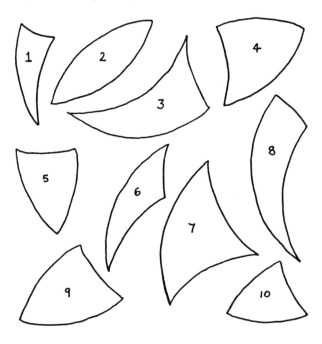

And the answer is:

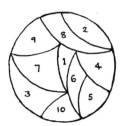

Chapter

3

WORLD OF ACTIVITIES

July 4th Celebration Games....56:(Bell Toss 56; States' Shuffleboard 57)

Gooly-Dunda...58

Hopscotch...58:(The Fossil 59; Aeroplane 59)

April Fools' Games....59:(Odd Art Competition 60; Pigs Can Fly 61; Weird Objects 61)

Battling Tops....61

Things with String....63:(Moon 65; Eskimo House 65)

Fighting Kites....66

Post Office Balls....68

Treasure Hunts....69:(Nigel's Hunt 69; Alan's Hunt 69)

Kabaddi....70

Hash Running....73

Quoits and Horseshoes....76:(Quoits 76; Horseshoes 77; Deck Quoits 78)

Chase Games 78:(Piggyback Tag 79; Bump Tag 79; Longy-della 79; Crows and Cranes 79; Monsters 80; Red Rover 80; Queeny, Kingy or Tag ball 81)

Wall Game....81

Weird Races....82:(Hoop Race 83; Back to Back Race 83; Scavenger Hunt 83; Frog or Rabbit Race 84; Other ideas for Races 84)

Hoppy Currie....85

Weigh Butter....85

Art Arena Games....86

Kick the Can....88

French Cricket....88

Greek Ball....89

Pulling the Rod....90

Three Way Tug of War....90

Coin Throwing....91:(Penny on the Drum 91; Brother Jonathan 91; Bottle Toss 92)

Jeu de Boules....92

KABADDI KABADDI.. ..KABADDI ... (Er....GULP!)

JULY 4TH CELEBRATION GAMES

In America, July 4th is the day when everyone celebrates the Declaration of Independence. The day has a carnival atmosphere and a lot of Americans who are living away from the States try to enjoy some sort of celebration wherever they happen to be. Part of that celebration can involve playing games, which John Adams, one of America's presidents, said should be part of the Fourth of July celebrations:

> to celebrate with..."pomp and parade, with shows, games, sports, guns, bells, bonfires and illuminations, from one end of this continent to the other."

We'd strongly recommend leaving out the guns!

A couple of games we have heard of are:

Bell Toss

Hang some sort of bell from the branch of a tree. Then use this as a target for participants to aim at with a tennis ball or similar. Ringing the bell scores a point, and for Americans provides an echo of the ringing of the Liberty Bell, which is rung each Independence Day, to commemorate the original bell at a Philadelphia courthouse in 1776. Participants should agree how many rounds of throws they are going to play.

States' Shuffleboard

This is best played on a pavement where target squares can be chalked without causing any annoyance to neighbours. The idea is to set out a board as in the illustration with five points being awarded for playing pieces which land in capital city/county town circles and one point for each counter falling inside state/county boundaries (not touching a line). Draw on the ground between a dozen and twenty area squares including the circles. Players use a broom or hockey stick to propel the playing pieces, which can be jam jar lids or similar. We used five playing pieces for each player's turn. Agree at the outset how many goes each player is going to have.

You can either use this as a way of getting the players to look at a map of the United States and learn some of the state names and those of capitals, or you can turn it into a UK game with counties or regions, and major towns and cities. In its most elaborate form, the outlines of the states/counties can be refined to look like the shape of the actual areas involved. This is a good party game, but is flexible enough for almost any situation where an 'active' game is required.

GOOLY-DUNDA

Also spelled 'Gilli Danda.'

Douglas, who we met while we were in Goa, wasn't able to show us this game in action, but it provided a lot of entertainment when we got back to the UK, first in trying to make a simple set, and then trying it out. We have since realised that Alan played a pub game in Kent called 'Bat and Trap' which was definitely a UK relation of 'Gooly-Dunda.' There are also regional games in different parts of the UK which resemble Gooly Dunda. In Wales there is 'Twyn Shwm Catti,' from Scotland, 'Tip Cat,' where the 'cat' is the stick which is hit, and in Yorkshire, 'Knurr and Spell,' which is a traditional street game involving hitting a small ball propelled out of a trap.

Anyway, Gooly-Dunda can easily be constructed, or can be played using found materials. The person with the bat stands in a particular spot which is defined as the wicket. The bat is any large stick which is reasonably smooth. We ended up with a piece of wood a bit like a scaled down stoolball bat, just under two feet long. The missile to be struck is a tapered stick, (you need a small stock of these), each about six inches long. The rules of the game are extremely simple. As in cricket, there is a batting team and a bowling/fielding team. The batter places the stick on top of another piece of wood and hits one end. This propels the stick into the air, and the batter then re-hits the stick, trying to propel it as far as possible without being caught out.

Variations can obviously include allowing the batter up to three attempts to make a hit before having to make a run, which can be up to a convenient post, tree or suchlike. Alternatively, we have found that the value of a hit can be determined purely on distance, therefore making running unnecessary. This can be a popular alternative to cricket, rounders or stoolball, and teams can be anything from one-a-side up to about ten or twelve on each team.

HOPSCOTCH

The variations and permutations of hopscotch games seem endless. Despite its British sounding name, it is a form of game which has been played by children around the world for centuries; it is known as *Marelles* in France, *Ekaria Dukaria* in India, and *Tempelhüpfen* in Germany. In fact it is played just about everywhere in Europe, including Russia, and throughout North America and China. A really universal game.

Because it is a street or playground game, the rules vary enormously as children use it as an opportunity to experiment and make up their own game. However, certain aspects are common to all the games. A scotch is a line, and the aim of the game is to hop around a course chalked on the ground, without touching any of the lines. Apart from chalk the only other piece of equipment used in most games is a small stone, which is usually flat, and in some countries is called the 'potsie.' The potsie, or marker stone is used in a number of games to indicate how far a player has reached either by hopping (always on the same foot), or by a combination of hopping and kicking the stone.

We would recommend that you encourage children to invent their own versions, since it is a good opportunity for using the imagination. Just to get you started we have included two slightly unusual variants, which Ron, from Abercynon in South Wales, remembered from his youth. The game is known as 'peevers' in Howie's native Scotland!

The Fossil

Also known as the 'Snail' or 'French Hop.' The game is chalked out as follows:

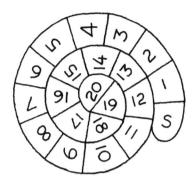

The first player puts the stone down in the start area and on one foot kicks it into number one and then hops in to the number after it. This sequence is repeated, moving from number one into number two and so on. If the player's foot touches a line, or the stone stops on a line, or goes outside of the playing area, the player is out. If the player successfully reaches number 20 they are then 'killer,' and they re-start at the beginning. Wherever they now reach they chalk the square with their initial, which is 'killed' for other players who must hop over it.

Aeroplane

This is a tricky pattern which requires some big hops between numbers. In this game players first have to hop through the sequence of numbers, then return back to the start. For subsequent rounds, the potsie is carried, while hopping, firstly on the elevated foot, then on the head, shoulder etc..

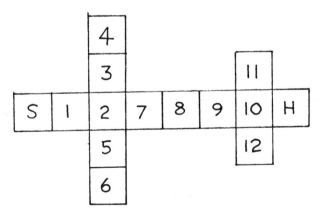

APRIL FOOLS' GAMES

Back in the sixteenth century, the French introduced a new calendar which moved New Year's Day from April to January. News travelled very slowly and many people in France went on celebrating New Year in April and were consequently called April Fools.

If you run a club or youth group of some kind, it may be fun to try running a silly April Fools' Night celebration. Ideas we have had include:

- Getting everybody to dress up in confused clothing, odd socks, wrong gender clothes, hair that has two colours or whatever.
- Organising a meal where the courses were served in the wrong order starting with the sweet course. The adults greeted the youngsters as they arrived by saying, "Goodbye." Before and after the meal we organised some very stupid and silly games, such as the following:

Odd Art Competition

First, prepare some small cards or bits of paper with the names of simple objects on them, such as scissors, a hat, a telephone, a fork etc.. Hand out sheets of paper to all the participants and a felt pen or a biro. This is when the fun begins; distribute one card to each player and ask them to draw their object with the hand they don't usually use! Try to make sure that the other players do not see what is written on the cards.

This game does not need to be competitive, but it is fun to find out how many people can recognise the objects which have been created. The results tend to be quite bizarre.

Pigs Can Fly

The games organiser for this sequence explains that they will start off the game by calling out short phrases which are either true or false. A true statement is followed by two claps from all of the people in the group. A false statement is followed by silence. The trick is to keep the sequence moving fast. For instance, the sequence might start with "cats have fur" (clap, clap); then "fish can swim" (clap, clap); then "pigs can fly"....which may be greeted by silence, or, if anyone claps they become the next group leader.

This sequence can be used in a variety of settings and is fun in both 'serious' groupwork or informal party situations. With younger groups, the adults may have to do most of the leading since the young ones may find it hard to think of suitable sentences.

Weird Objects

We met up with this game at an education centre in a nature park. The idea is to organise a number of bags which you cannot see through, each containing one object. Participants take it in turn to feel the object and guess what it is. Most people think that the object is more horrible than it really is, and objects such as a peeled orange, a banana skin, a pine cone, or a ping pong ball can produce a varied range of 'guesses.'

BATTLING TOPS

We met up with this in India, and believe that it is still popular in both Bombay and Calcutta. It possibly originated, though, from the Chinese populations based in India. We were familiar with spinning tops in our own childhood, but the Indian variety have a sharper metal spike on which they revolve. Tops can still be bought from some stores in the UK which specialise in selling traditional wooden games.

To make this type of top spin requires a little practice! We were shown how to do it by a man in his early thirties named Anthony and he told us that he had been a champion in his youthful years. He certainly made it look easy! As in the following drawing, the cord is tied round the neck of the top, in some cases following the grooves made in the wood. The loose end of the cord is held while throwing the top towards the ground, which, if you are lucky or are becoming skilful, will make the top spin vigorously.

Skilled top-spinners can also lift the top up on to a finger, move it through the air onto a flattened palm and toss it, still spinning, between hands. But this is not the aim of the traditional competitive game. In 'Battling tops,' two players throw their tops to the ground at the same time and the aim is to own the last top still spinning. When the tops nudge into each other, usually one top comes off best. Eventually one stops before the other and is declared the loser. In some cases the top spinning takes place within a roped off circle. We have also used a plastic hoola-hoop to contain the contest.

Early in this century the Bombay tops also had a long nail, pointed at both ends, driven horizontally through the top. With these tops, the aim was literally to destroy the opponent's playing piece. The winner was the top still left intact! We do not recommend re-instating the twin-pointed nail, but it is interesting to see how games have been 'toned-down' over time.

There are also competitions which involve landing the top on to some sort of game board or chalk marked layout on the ground.

Version One involves trying to land the top on a particular point on the ground. The player scores the number of points indicated, scoring highest (10 points) for landing the top on the intersection.

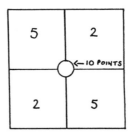

Variation Two involves each player landing their tops onto the playing zone and trying to kill their opponent's top in a 'no-score' area. Each top then scores the value of the zone where it finally comes to rest.

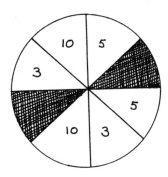

THINGS WITH STRINGS

Producing figures with string is an ancient pastime. In a 1930s book, 'Artists in String' Kathleen Haddon said:

> "The making of string figures is one of the oldest of the arts, the most universal of games, the most puzzling (in its geographical distribution) of all the queer things that primitive people do."

To us, writing this book towards the end of twentieth century, the manipulation of string to create complex patterns, sequences and shapes has nothing 'primitive' about it. Very happily it is still an activity which can be enjoyed by young people, but it is certainly helped along a bit by some knowledge of shapes which can be created and where they came from.

These days, anyone who has even heard of string figures automatically refers to them as 'cat's cradles,' even though that is only one of the many 'figures' which can be manipulated. What we'd like to offer in this short section are a few string figures which can be made with a little patience and practice. We also offer a short introduction to where these figures originally come from (as far as we can work it out)!

A Knotted (Sorry, potted) history of string figures!

The geographical locations where string figures have been located proves that they are one of the most widespread pre-occupations of early civilisations. The earliest figures seem to have come from the far north of the Arctic region of America, with a range of examples emanating from Alaska and around the Behring Sea. Further south off South America, the Guianas in the Caribbean have produced some interesting examples. Most of the African states have popularised a variety of figures, likewise Australia, New Zealand, Papua, Hawaii, the Philippines and the New Hebrides. Europe and India have relatively little tradition of string figures, despite the well-known, supposedly English two-player 'Cat's Cradle.' In fact, this probably originated in either the Pacific islands or China and is likely to have been introduced to the UK through world trade.

What has always puzzled those interested in string figures, is, what are they? It is by no means clear. Are they symbolic, religious artefacts, children's amusements, simple representations of 'real life' as a primitive art form? Strangely, the one purpose they appear to have consistently performed is to be a form of communication between different races and cultures. That's one of the reasons we thought that they should be included in this particular book. They are also fun to be involved with, tactile, and do help break down barriers between people. Apparently there is a long tradition of explorers and missionaries using their skill at manipulating string as a means of 'breaking the ice' with people from other cultures. Again quoting Haddon:

> "The effect is magical. Instead of hanging back or hiding in hut and bush, the natives cluster eagerly round. Shyness is forgotten: each vies with each in showing new figures."

For our purposes here, that is probably enough about their origins, suffice it to say that anthropologists continue to puzzle over how similarly shaped string figures turn up in civilisations separated by thousands of miles of ocean. Not only are the shapes similar, but so too the manipulations, sometimes contortions, which are necessary to make the more intricate configurations. Anyway, in the following pages are a few string figures for you to try and to share with young people.

Getting started

To start making string figures you'll need enough cut lengths of string, each about 6ft 6ins long. The best string is smooth and flexible, something like picture cord is best. The string needs to be joined as a continuous loop, tied together as a reef knot, sewn together with cotton, or, best of all, spliced. Frequently, the figure, the pattern you are trying to make, is in the centre of the web of string, rather than being represented by the whole web. This is clear in the first figure which is meant to represent the oval shaped shell of the Fly-River Turtle, known to the Navaho Indians. (however, we won't try to explain the construction of this shape as it seemed a bit too complex for us!)

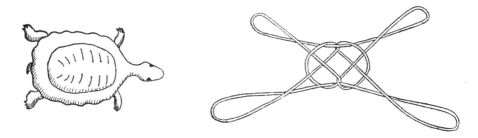

The difficulty in simply describing how to construct string games almost put us off including them in this book (which would have been a pity!). Kathleen Haddon and her main collaborator, Dr Rivers, were both academics and whilst they had a passion for string figures and the anthropological links with different cultures they did tend to complicate matters. We decided to identify the various fingers on each hand and then to list as bullet points the sequence of moves required to make the various shapes. We are indebted to J.B. Pick, whose Armada book '100 games for one player' makes the descriptions about as simple as they can be.

The use of the word 'nearer' means nearer to the player's body.

There appears to be a standard starting position, and an almost as common opening position, which we illustrate next:

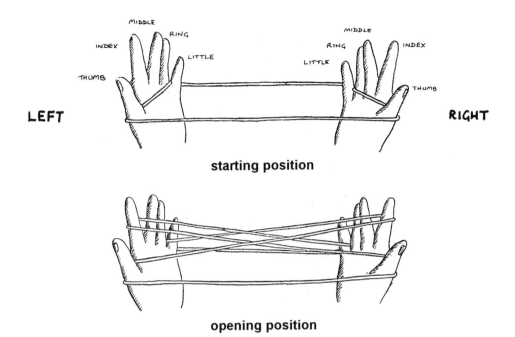

starting position

opening position

Moon

We think that this moon shape may have come from Australia where the moon is seen as the symbol of the man, who has two wives, the summer sun and the winter sun.

- *From the opening position take the furthest away string in the mouth thereby releasing the loops from the little fingers on both hands. Be sure not to tighten up the other string loops.*
- *Take the thumb loops onto the two little fingers by inserting the little fingers from above into the thumb loops.*
- *Insert both index fingers into the bottom of the loop held in the mouth. This means that there are two loops now on the index fingers.*
- *Finally, slip the lower string off from the index fingers and then draw out the figure, which should leave you with the following:*

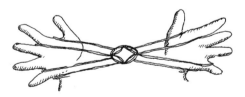

Eskimo House

Alaskan Eskimos believed (and may still believe) in the 'spirit' of string figures. Making string figures was seen as a way of protecting their home and their family from any negative influence of the spirit which was believed could paralyse and even kill.

- *From the opening position, turn the two palms towards you.*

- *Close the fingers of both hands over all the loops, except the one nearest you, then twist this string over the backs of both hands.*
- *Return hands to their 'normal' position with palms facing each other.*
- *There should now be a new string which passes across the backs of the hands, runs straight between the hands on the little finger side and forms a cross on the thumb side.*
- *Pass the thumbs over this near the back of the hand string, and below all the other strings.*
- *With the backs of both thumbs, hook off the further back of the hand string and then return to the usual hands position.*
- *Finally, slip off the loops from the backs of the hands over the fingers onto the palm and extend to form the Eskimo house:*

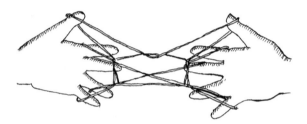

Whilst we have described string figures as a single player 'game,' cats' cradles are frequently made by two people working together swapping the shape from one person's hands to the others, which allows for complicated manipulation of the string.

FIGHTING KITES

In China, Korea, Japan and India, the use of 'fighting kites' is a widespread pastime. We encountered kites being used in competitive airborne 'fights' in Bihar, Gujarat and Bengal, but probably it is a pastime which can be enjoyed anywhere.

Indian and Chinese kites are home-made. A design for a simple one, which we happen to know has a reasonable chance of flying, is given below, from our own *Youth Arts and Craft Book*. Since the game we are explaining involves losing one of the kite's tails (and possibly the kite(s)) it is important not to use expensive or elaborate kites. In India, the use of square kites is very common, but in our strong UK winds, we have found them very unstable!

The aim of the game is for two players to make kites with tails and then to fly them at the same time in a battle. The section of string nearest the kite, say for four or five feet, as agreed beforehand, is coated with fine glass filings glued onto the string. This is sharp and can cut hands, so handle with care! Each participant flies their kite and tries to cut the opponent's tail off from the kite. Successfully achieving this scores a 'win'. In some cultures the aim is to actually detach the opponent's kite, but we like the extra sophistication of aiming to cut off the tail section.

Simple kite construction
This kite flies well in moderate to strong winds.

You will need:

2 spars of square section soft or hard wood, the lighter the better.
   one of 36 inches by a quarter of an inch
   one of 32 inches by a quarter of an inch
Lightweight cloth, newspaper, crepe or tissue paper 36 inches square.
Line with a 25 gms breaking strain minimum.
Glue and a towing ring (curtain ring, washer or similar).

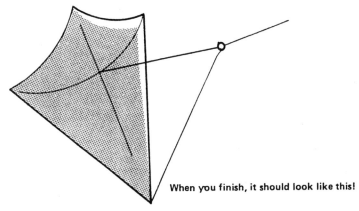

When you finish, it should look like this!

Using the long spar as the spine of the kite, tie the short spar to the spine 6 inches from the top to form a cross. Now, notch the ends of the spars and tie line round the frame (diagram 1).

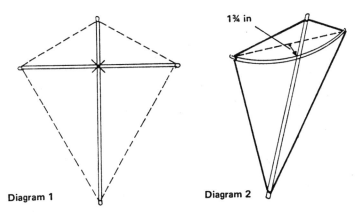

1¾ in

Diagram 1

Diagram 2

Cut out the cover, allowing enough of a hem to turn it over the frame, and glue it down. Next, tie a line tightly along the cross-spar to flex the kite. There should be roughly one and three-quarter inches clearance between the line and the spine.

Now strengthen two bridle points on the cover, approximately six inches from the top and two inches from the bottom of the kite. This can be done with paper reinforcing circles, or a piece of cloth or whatever with a small hole cut in it. Pierce a hole in the strengthened part of the kite and tie the bridle string around the bar behind. The string should be a total length of approximately 84 inches, and should be looped once through the towing ring. if you adjust the bridle so that the top part of it is roughly 36 inches long and the bottom part is 48 inches, then the kite will be set at the correct angle of attack for normal wind conditions. (Diagram 3).

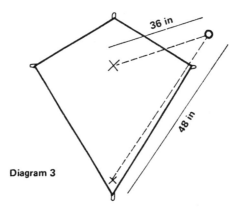

Diagram 3

Finally, attach the line to the towing ring. The ring will remain in position as you tighten the line and the bridle. A tail should be added at this point and needs to be between seven and nine feet long and made of very light material. Pieces of crepe paper, intertwined into the light string of the tail works well. The tail adds stability to the kite, as well as providing a target for the opposition! We managed to obtain glass filings from both a glass works and a specialist hobby shop.

POST OFFICE BALLS

You have the two ladies behind the post office counter at Lyme Regis Post Office down in deepest Dorset to thank for this little oddity. Imagine a wet January day, wind howling outside, sea lashing against the harbour walls, and no-one in sight in the swirling wastes of wintry Broad Street. Alan dived into the Post Office with his end of day parcels and hurtling towards him was a bouncy ball made entirely of rubber bands, courtesy of a very bored Estelle and Symphony, our very own Post Office Counters' Games Inventors. And, amidst lots of giggles, a second missile which resembled a large melon bounced its way over the protective shield!

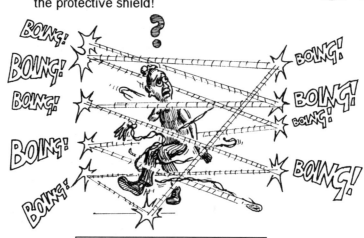

We subsequently purchased a couple of extremely large bags of elastic bands which are, incidentally, very cheap in the right kind of shop. We gave them out to a small group of seven and eight year olds, explaining that the object was to wrap the bands tightly around each other, gradually building up a tightly compacted rubber ball. The Post Office ball was easily able to bounce from the floor up to hit the roof, and sure enough, within half an hour, the group of youngsters had produced golf-ball sized versions of the Post Office ball. Some time later on, during an evening at a friend's house we repeated the exercise, this time convincing a mixed age group of four adults and three children aged 11 to 15 that making elastic band balls was the most exciting thing they could possibly do. By about ten o' clock that evening we had some very high bouncing, tennis ball sized creations.

TREASURE HUNTS

These are a universally popular pastime with young people (and indeed adults). We have used a variety of methods for organising treasure hunts with young people, but the first one described here comes from Nigel Clarke, who runs a publishing firm next door to Alan down in Dorset.

Nigel's Hunt

The aim behind Nigel's Treasure Hunt is to ensure that younger or slower children still have a chance to win some treasure. What Nigel does is to:

- hide, either in a garden or inside a house a number of gift tags, which are tied to a variety of objects at different heights;
- instruct all the children to go and find the tags *one at a time* and bring them back to him;
- reward each child with one or more sweets for each tag they find.

This type of Treasure Hunt slows down the older or faster children and makes sure that the smaller children get plenty of prizes.

Alan's Hunt

Alan's Treasure Hunt is more complicated and is suited for adolescent groups. It works like this:

- Alan makes up a sheet of clues which will help the players to find the various solutions. He then photocopies a sheet for everyone taking part and keeps a copy with the solutions on it. At the start he explains that the clues can be tackled in any order, and that on the correct object there is a small sticker with a letter on it. These letters must be written in on the answer sheet.
- The types of clues he makes up vary in difficulty to suit the group. For instance, a

clue for a clock could be:

>Old Father.............
>
>>or
>
>It has two hands
>
>>or, for a particular book (Treasure Island) it might be:
>
>Pieces of Eight
>
>>or
>
>Look for Long John Silver.

- On the clock, or whatever, Alan puts a small sticker (being careful not to damage the item it is being stuck to!) Players are told that they must not remove any of the stickers.
- If there are eighteen clues, this will give eighteen letters. Alan's clue sheet has a final clue on it which might be:

>>You would find them in the kitchen.

- The letters corresponding to all the clues have been jumbled up, but can be re-arranged to make up a series of words which is the name of items to be found in the kitchen:

>>e.g. table and four chairs.

It is best to have a time limit for this type of Treasure Hunt, and if there are some younger children involved, pair them up with older participants. A harder variation of the above is to have one clue leading to the next, but this has the disadvantage that everyone is trying to find the same answers at the same time and may start to spy on the faster players.

KABADDI

Kabaddi is slowly becoming a popular game in the UK, partly as a result of active promotion by the National Kabaddi Association (UK), and partly through the Channel 4 coverage of the Kabaddi league from India. The name for the game varies throughout Asia and the sub-continent. It is variously known as 'Kabaddi' in India and Pakistan, 'Do-Do' in Nepal, 'Guddo' in Sri Lanka, 'Technib' in Indonesia and 'Kaudi,' 'Zabar,' 'Sonchi,' and Bhaddi-Bhaddi' in other areas. What is common to all versions of the game is that it requires no ball, and no equipment other than a reasonably flat playing area marked out as either a rectangle or circle.

Makhdoom Ahmad Chishti, the National Development Officer for the Kabaddi Association (UK) kindly helped us put together the following information about the game. He says of the game:

>*"The basis of Kabaddi lies in attacking and defending territory as well as overcoming the opponent. The players are called raiders and defenders. The beauty of the game is that players attack and defend at the same time. Physical strength and mental agility are the main qualities of a good Kabaddi player."*

The Birmingham Pakistan Sports Forum, together with the Sports Council, have taken a lead role to develop awareness of the game at local and national level in the UK. Within this strategy, they are keen to see Kabaddi introduced into schools, and are positively working to develop versions of the game which are suitable for children, women and girls, and people with disabilities.

To a western pair of eyes the game looks like a mixture of tag and rugby, but minus the ball! Gradually the game has evolved from a rural village game into a sport with specific rules governing all aspects of play and the size of the playing area. However, because there are two distinct sets of rules which apply to the two different playing courts, the rectangular and circular, it is impossible to offer one definitive version of Kabaddi.

If you want to get involved in league competitions, and therefore require the full set of rules, we suggest that you contact the National Kabaddi Association at 7 Rolling Mill Close, Edgbaston, Birmingham, B5 7QD.

To play

We have decided for space limitations to describe the basic rules of the Rectangular Kabaddi. Marking out a rectangle is easier than a circle, and using an indoor badminton court equipped with matting makes a good, impromptu Kabaddi pitch. We have also slightly simplified the adult pitch, leaving out the gallery lines.
The pitch is marked out (if possible) as follows:

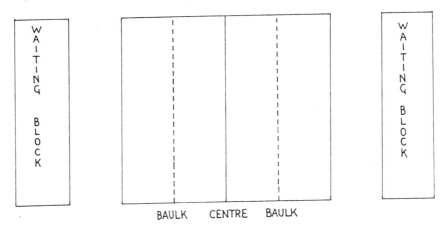

The dimensions for the pitch are: 13 metres x 10 metres for men, and 10 metres by 8 metres for women and younger players.

The pitch is divided in two by the centre line and then each team's court is further divided in two by the baulk line. (In the adult pitch, on either side of the playing court is a metre wide corridor, called the gallery). Completely outside of the playing court, at each end of the pitch, is a waiting block, where players who have been forced to temporarily leave the game await their return.

A game lasts thirty minutes and there is a five minute break at half time. Each team consists of twelve players, five of whom are 'reserves.' One member of each team takes a turn to make a raid into the defender's court. During a raid, the raider must:

- not take a breath and must continuously chant, "kabaddi, kabaddi, kabaddi;"
- cross over the defender's baulk line at least once;
- try to touch defenders, and
- return to their own court without losing their 'chant.' (kabaddi, kabaddi)

The aim of the game is to score points which is achieved by making successful 'raids' into the opposing team's court, and by successfully defending, tackling incoming raiders and preventing them from returning.

A productive raid is one where a raider manages to touch one or more defenders with any part of their body and return to their own court while continuing the chant. On the raider's successful return, all the defenders who have been touched must move to the waiting block. **An unproductive raid** is one where the raider fails to touch a defender. Confusingly, **an unsuccessful raid** is one where the raider loses a point through losing the chant, fails to cross the baulk line, or steps out of the court. In each case that raider must then go to the waiting block.

Other comments on scoring:

- After a productive raid, every defender who was touched must leave the court and move to the waiting block, even if they were touched when trying to make a catch.
- If a raider is tackled (held in the defender's court until the chant is broken) the defending team wins a point.
- If all the defenders are touched and sent to the waiting block, this scores a **Lona**, which gives two points to the raiding team. Play then re-commences with all the seven defending players coming back into the playing court.
- If a team carries out three unproductive raids in a row this gives the defending team a bonus point.

Tactics and other comments on play:

The game is always played bare footed and in the Indian male-version, only shorts are worn. However, in the UK, the move is towards standardising the game, with all players wearing shirts. Among prohibited tactics are for players to kick, bite, punch, head butt, strangle and generally *"apply any holds which may endanger the opponent's life or cause a fracture or dislocation......."*

The captain of either side may make a substitute when there is an injury or when they wish to bring on a new player. Once substituted, a player is out of the game. The captain can concede a Lona in order to bring back a full strength team.

Players can be 'revived,' i.e. brought back into the playing area from the waiting block when:

-a defending team successfully catches a raider;
-a raider makes a productive raid which frees an equal number of the raider's team members from the waiting zone.

At full time in competitions, if the team scores are level the teams play for an extra ten minutes, switching ends after five minutes.

Neither of us have had the chance of taking part in a Kabaddi game. We wonder if it is possible to organise mixed games of boys and girls, or whether the physical strength aspect of the game means that the male and female versions of the game need to be segregated? Time and experience will provide the answers, no doubt.

HASH RUNNING

The description of this activity is very similar to the one Alan and his mate, Dave Kelf, used in Alan Smith's book, 'Creative Outdoor Work with Young People.' (Russell House Publishing, 1994) Hash Running is a much travelled activity, but was first developed in the Far East by British servicemen and workers. A gentleman called Gisbert was the original hasher. Since then it has been re-imported back into the UK and every other part of the world. Throughout the British Isles alone there are many clubs often called the such and such Hash House Harriers (sometimes shortened to H3). Alan, together with Dave and young and (older) colleagues from Axe Valley Runners in Devon run in informally organised hash runs a few times every year. So, what is it all about?

The basic idea has evolved from the paper chase, but is much better for mixed ability running groups, and more ecologically sound! It also provides a very positive experience for young people, who may not want to 'compete' in running events, and may even dread their cross-country run at school!

To organise a hash event, a volunteer agrees to lay one or more hash trails from a given starting point, usually a sports' clubhouse, where the 'hashers' will gather at a pre-arranged time. The trail is marked with small piles of sand, flour or sawdust on tracks, paths and roadways. These are usually placed at fairly regular intervals, say every hundred metres. The faster runners follow the trail until they come to a 'check' sign with arrows pointing in several directions. This denotes a number of choices, and the lead runners share the task of 'checking' perhaps three or four trails which have been laid from the intersection point. Tradition is that they call back "On On" to the runners behind them when they've found a continuous trail. This message is relayed back through the pack. If uncertain they call back 'checking' and "On Two," "On Three" etc., BUT, only one trail is correct and after a few hundred metres the runners on the false trails will find themselves confronted with a sawdust 'X', and they yell "False Trail" or "Check back." They then have to run back to the intersection and pick up the correct trail.'

It is the false trails that act as the balancing factor since they ensure that the lead runners do extra mileage, and it gives the proverbial 'tortoise' the chance to catch up with the 'hares.' Whenever there is a main road intersection, or after a longish stretch, the hash organiser marks the ground with an 'H' or 'R,' which means 'Hold' or 'Halt' or 'Re-group.' This allows all the hash participants to re-group, and allows a safety check to see that no-one has gone missing. Eventually the trail returns the hashers back to the starting point, with the leader calling an "On home" instruction. All in all it is a very sociable form of running.

Quite often, the organiser will set short and long trails, of perhaps four and eight miles, which allow the runners with extra stamina to put in extra miles, whilst providing a more leisurely course for the less experienced, or there may be 'approved' short cuts. No map reading is used, and most hash clubs are a mix of wizened veteran runners, young

teenagers, dogs, keep fit enthusiasts and a scattering of serious athletes who understand the training value of hash running across country. For groups of young people it can offer a good mixture of country path rambling, running and companionable fun. As long as the organiser has a good knowledge of footpaths and bridleways and keeps away from main roads, this can provide a couple of hours healthy outdoor entertainment. Often a hash is organised from a pub which is willing to 'enjoy' the company of a mixed age group of muddy joggers later in the evening. Alan recently saw a runner with, 'On Inn' emblazoned on the back of his T-shirt!

A few tips:

1. It is best that the hash organiser runs with the hash to ensure that folk do not get horribly lost, possibly because a 'mark' has been obliterated. It is useful to have a reliable back marker who can act as 'sweeper'.
2. In fields where there are a lot of young cattle or sheep, the runners may need to slow down or walk to avoid panicking the livestock. It is important that the organiser should warn landowners of the event in advance.
3. Especially on hot days or evenings, it is a good idea if the organiser sets up a drinks container and paper cups at one of the halts at about the half way point. Sweating can cause quite bad dehydration.
4. If the organiser puts on a 'bum bag' they can carry a whistle, a small first aid kit and a map, all of which may prove useful.

5. Hashers should always follow the Country Code, particularly shutting gates.

6. Laying a trail is great fun, but requires map reading skills and a desire to 'out guess' the faster runners!

7. Someone should have responsibility for car keys or leave them with someone at the base.

8. A good hash route will take in lots of different types of terrain, preferably including mud and some water!

Tradition.

Part of the fun of hashing is its quirky rules and traditions! Often the organising committee have distinctive titles: Grand Master; Grand Mistress; Hash Cash; On Sec; Religious Advisor and Hash Horn. Individual hashers also gain Hash Handles, which are not always too complimentary!

Hash Runners are particularly active in fund raising for charities. They also organise local events and runs, print up special T-shirts and are increasingly family orientated. Every two years there is a UK Nash (National) Hash gathering, where many trails are set and much celebration takes place. This includes alternative Hash events such as Wibbly Wobbly races and 'Down Downs.'

Altogether, it's about having FUN above all else.

QUOITS AND HORSESHOES

We were intrigued to see that Quoits is a sport recognised by the Sports Council, so we contacted Alan Burton, the Secretary of the National Quoits Association to find out more about the sport. Alongside this, we talked to a number of people who played, or play, Quoits or the North American equivalent, 'Horseshoes.' We also consulted a number of modern and older books. The outcome is this entry on a number of throwing games which can be played quite successfully with young people. Quoits and Horseshoes require accurate throwing, whilst 'Deck Quoits' needs agility and catching skills as well.

No-one really knows where the Quoits or Horseshoe games have come from. Some people reckon that they evolved from Greek discus throwing; others speculate that they developed from soldiers' games, perhaps Roman in origin. Since variations of the game are popular in South Africa, Holland and Canada, there are very conflicting views on who 'invented' the game. In the UK, the games are played in little pockets of activity. Quoits seems centred in the North-east of England, the Borders and Central Regions of Scotland, and either side of the Welsh border around Herefordshire and in Powys and Dyfed.

The original spelling of Quoits was 'Coits' and it's up to you to take your choice on whether Horseshoes or Quoits is the older game. The earliest reference to the game we found was 1361, when Edward III tried to outlaw the game on the basis that it was interfering with his soldiers' archery practise.

Quoits

The rules for Quoits are fairly simple, but rather too specific for use with groups of young people.

In the nationally recognised game, each player has two quoits which are specially made by blacksmiths from iron and are not more than 5.25 lbs, less than 1.25" thick, and less than 8.5" outer and 5.5" inner diameter. These missiles have a curved upper side and a flat bottom. For the purposes of youth groups, we have improvised using almost anything that is roughly this shape, but usually a lot lighter in weight. We have also scaled down the throwing distance of 11 yards. You need to try it with the particular group you are playing with and see how far they can throw accurately. We have played the game on beaches, playgrounds and parks using rubber rings of different colours, over a range of about fifteen to twenty feet.

We have tried to keep the rules fairly close to the national standard, but you are unlikely to have the need for two, three foot square clay beds with a hob or pin in each one. The pin or hob at each end is the target, and it is supposed to be a pin of no more than half an inch diameter, which projects up to three inches out of the ground. Some of the other rules are also a bit particular to be necessary for playing with young people, unless their aim is to join in the local Quoits' League. Our game is akin to 'Sward Quoits' or 'Grass Quoits,' which is a more informal variety of the national game. We have used anything from a tent peg, a cricket stump through to a fence post for our 'hob.' The quoits we use are made of rubber and can be bought from some beach goods stores and pet shops.

The play and scoring involves each player throwing their two quoits (usually clearly marked to identify them) from the area of one hob towards the one at the other end. Once all the quoits have been thrown, scoring takes place:

- A quoit which has gone over the hob is called a 'ringer' and each scores two points if they belong to the same player. If the player's two ringers are divided by an opponent's quoit, only the top quoit scores. If there are one quoit each for two players only the top quoit scores.
- The two quoits landing nearest the hob count one point each if they belong to the same player or side. If they belong to opposing sides, then only the nearest quoit scores the one point score.
- Two or more quoits which are touching the hob are deemed to be equal. These are called 'leaners' by some players and often score one point.
- A game usual lasts until one player or team has scored 21 points.

In a sense it is a shame to lose the local names for the throws and the ways in which the quoits land; a 'black pot', a 'hole gater' etc. sound very indicative of the working class roots of this game. The National Quoits Association are still battling to get their game accepted into the Olympics, but we suspect it will be a long fight!

Horseshoes

In North America, the game of 'Horseshoes' is regarded as a folksy, rural pastime, which George Bush, amongst other US Presidents tried to popularise. For the children's version of the game, two target stakes are driven into the ground, 20' apart (instead of 40' for adult males, 30' for females). Lighter horseshoes are usually used for pitching by children than the regulation two and a half pound.

The play and scoring involves either two players or two teams of two. In singles play, each player pitches both their horseshoes, which are distinctively coloured, then the other person pitches.
- The aim, as in Quoits, is to get the horseshoes onto the spike, which scores three points each for a 'ringer.'
- The closest horseshoe to the stake, including a 'leaner' scores one point, and if the player's second horseshoe is also closer than the opponent's second horseshoe they score a further point.
- The maximum score for an innings is six points.
- The usual winning game score is 21 points for doubles and 50 for singles.

We have been recommended by American friends not to try playing the game with children under ten unless they are very responsible and reasonably co-ordinated. Flying horseshoes can be lethal!

Deck Quoits

The varieties of 'Deck Quoits' have mostly evolved from the game played on board the great cruise ships of the inter-war years. On the Queen Elizabeth, the Queen Mary, the Nevassa and the Delwara, Deck Quoits were a favourite form of whiling away the time and getting some exercise. However, it has also been a popular game for primary schools, requiring very little in the way of equipment, and helping to develop good eye and hand co-ordination. As a game for young people and children, it is fun, easy to learn and the rules can be adapted to the surroundings, available equipment and the age and skill of the participants.

The game can be played by two players, or by two teams of two or three players.

Play and scoring.

The game requires one rubber quoit and some sort of net. The ground is marked out with chalk, or you can use the lines from a badminton court to define the area of play if you want to formalise the game.

- The way we have played it is to have the server throw the quoit horizontally standing behind the baseline, so that it does not wobble in the air and crosses over the net without touching it.
- A volley continues as long as one player on each side of the net continues to catch the quoit and throw it back.
- As soon as the quoit is dropped, the serve changes to a player on the opposing team.
- A point is only scored on the serve. So, for instance, if the server drops the quoit during a volley, they lose the serve but do not give away a point.
- Players take it in turns (in pairs or threes) to serve when it is their team's turn.
- Touching the top of the net with the quoit (where it continues over) or throwing a wobbly quoit is a 'let,' and the serve is re-taken.
- A game is won when one team or player reaches 15 points.

CHASE GAMES

Chase games are universal. 'Touching,' 'Tagging' and 'Having' are the common terms for the process of being caught. The Opies in their 'Children's Games in street and playground' book (Oxford University Press 1969) said,

> "chasing games could well be termed contaminating games were it not that the children themselves do not, on the whole, think of the chaser's touch as being strange or contagious."

In the 1950s, after a particular Goon show about the 'Lurgy' striking Britain, it was the 'lurgy' that was passed on between chasers and caught in the playgrounds. Likewise, in Valencia the ordinary game of tag is known as 'Tu portes la pusa' - you've got fleas! The person doing the chasing is often referred to by the impersonal title: 'It.' The rules of these games are hardly ever written down, except by adult historians. For children, the way in which the games were played seems to have been almost transmitted through the genes. They just knew how to play the various chasing games. Now, a lot of that knowledge seems to be lost and it becomes necessary, tedious as it appears, for adults to learn some of the rules of a few games and encourage active participation.

One of the most basic rules, common to many of the games is that the person who touches or tigs another, cannot immediately be tigged back. This rule applies across the continent as well as in the UK. German children will yell, "Widerschalach gildet nich" and in France, "ne peut rependre son pere."

For youth workers, playleaders and teachers, as well as adults charged with the job of organising a party, we hope the following may be useful. Rules are very flexible for this type of game and children should be encouraged to improvise. One other factor to bear in mind is the level of pushing, shoving and general physicality you think is reasonable. There is no simple answer. If your group spans a wide age range try to encourage participants to take care of the smaller and more vulnerable players. And, if you don't want to be chased yourself by irate parents, make sure the youngsters are wearing their old clothes.

Piggy-back tag

We heard of this one from an American friend who thought that our own piggy-back fighting game was rather too violent. As in piggy-back fights, players pair up, one climbing on the back of the other. On to the back of the riders, the organiser sticks a small 'tail' of masking tape. The aim is then for the horses and riders to chase each other and for the riders to capture the masking tape strips off their opponents. The last one left with a piece of tape intact wins. As you probably know, this is very similar to the 'fighting' version where riders try to pull and push other riders off their mounts until there is only one piggy-back team left. This used to be called 'Pick-a-back' or 'Collie-back' fighting.

Bump tag

This game isn't as dangerous as the title implies. We have found it particularly good for young groups, but it does need at least ten players. As in many tag games, there is no single winner since players keep changing roles.

All the participants divide up into groups of three, with the three being joined together by holding each other's waists. Any other players are 'it' and chase the teams of three with the aim of joining on to the back of any of the teams. If they are successful they yell, "Bump" and the player at the front of the threesome is freed to become a chaser. Ideally the game should continue until everyone has been 'it.'

Longy-della

Thirty years ago in the valleys of South Wales, Ron tells us that the most popular playground game was 'Longy-della.' No, he doesn't know what it means! Rather it is reminiscent of games played in the villages and small towns which still have annual competitions involving the whole population in a physical struggle through the streets, such as the Stonemasons' football match at Purbeck Maltravers or the Uppies and Downies in Jedburgh. Anyway, in Longy-della, teams of twenty or thirty line up facing one another, each with a wall, fence or railing behind them as their goal. On 'go' both teams try to reach their opponent's wall (or whatever) and each team tries to stop the other team members reaching their own wall. We suspect that it was good for rugby training!

Crows and Cranes

This is a bit like 'Longy-della,' but involves teams running way from each other instead of trying to barge their way past each other. It requires a games organiser or caller. We have heard it called different things in different places. Crows and Cranes is the common American name, but in the UK it is also known as Crusts and Crumbs. It is played in any outdoor area where there is a centre line and two baselines. The two teams should start off by being roughly equal in size; you need at least three a side for a game to be any fun. On a pitch of about twenty metres length, the 'crows' and the 'cranes' face one another across the centre line about three metres apart. The organiser calls out either 'cranes' or 'crows' and that team quickly turn round and run towards their 'home' line or wall. The other team members are in hot pursuit and any one tagged by them joins their team in the next round. Since the game is not meant to be too competitive, the organiser should try to vary round the calls for 'crows' and 'cranes' to give both teams a fair chance.

Monsters

Young friends of Alan's, Billie and Alex, decided that Alan would make a wonderful monster for this tag game! The game was played in their quite large garden and three areas were designated as 'safe' from intruding monsters. On the cry of 'Monster,' Alan had to run round the tracks in the garden like a demented Troll, trying to capture one of the nice children, who he kept threatening with, "eat them up, yum!" Once one of the children was lifted up in his arms, they belonged to the monster for about five minutes and had to help him capture a few more children. In Billie's Taunton version there were only three children and one monster, but played by about ten people, perhaps with two monsters to eight children, and with a time limit of say, only two minutes stay in a safe zone, this can make a fun little activity game, especially for under tens.

Red Rover

This is one of the most common and popular of the tag games in the world. However, the rules vary enormously. It can either be played with two teams of about ten or with a group of players and one 'caller.'

Version one with the caller:

In this version all the players stand at opposite ends of a defined playing area. The caller stands in the middle of the playing area and has three calls. In the first call they say: "Red Rover, Red Rover send---------over." The named person then tries to run to the other end of the playing area without being touched by the caller. If they are caught they remain 'captured' in the caller's den. If they are successful, they continue to take part. On the second call, a different runner's name is called, then on the third round, the caller says, "Red Rover, Red Rover, send them **all** over" and everyone has to change ends and try to avoid being caught.

Version with two teams:

In this version, two teams stand facing one another with their hands linked. Each team has a chosen leader. Teams take it in turn to call out, "Red Rover, Red Rover, send--------over," naming one member of the opposing team. That player must then try to break the chain and reach the other side of the chain. If they are stopped, they join the defending chain; if they succeed, they take back the two people from where the chain broke to join the other team. When one team has nearly run out of players, the sides are re-organised and the game re-started.

Queeny, Kingy or Tag ball

This is a bit like 'Dodge Ball' which we included in the *New Youth Games Book*, but it includes essential elements of the tag chasing game. It requires at least ten players and a soft ball or tennis ball. A chaser is chosen to start and the boundary of play is agreed.

- All the players scatter while the chaser bounces the ball ten times.
- While they are the only chaser they are allowed to move around with the ball as long as they bounce it on the ground. Their aim is to throw the ball to hit players (tag them) either below the waist or below the knees, depending on what rule has been agreed.
- Anyone hit becomes an 'It' as well and throws the ball at those being chased. Once there are more than one 'It', they must throw the ball from where they pick it up, but they can pass between themselves.
- Those being chased can run around as much as they like within the playing area, and can use fists to defend their bodies, however, if they fist the ball they can be caught out.
- Play continues until only one player is left being chased and they are declared King or Queen.
- The King or Queen usually chooses the next chaser.

If this doesn't resemble the playground or street game you half remember from your youth, apologies, but there are many, many local variations. Queeny is very popular in many regions of Scotland. In **one version** it is played with all the players standing in a circle. They try to keep the ball from hitting them by using their fists and they can catch it with their clenched fists and pass it to other players.

In a **second version** which Howie's children have played in the Borders, it is played either indoors or outdoors by younger groups of children, usually in a group of ten or more. One person is selected to be 'Queeny,' who stands at the front of the group, with their back to the group.

Queeny now takes the softball and throws it backwards - i.e. over the head, behind them towards the rest of the group. The player who catches the ball hides it behind their back and all the other players pretend to be hiding the ball behind their backs as well.

Once all the players are ready they shout: *"Queeny, Queeny, who has got the ball?"* Queeny now has three guesses to find out which player actually does have the ball behind their back. If Queeny guesses successfully, then the player who caught the ball becomes Queeny and the sequence starts again. If Queeny does not guess correctly, they have one more attempt at playing the game before they are out.

WALL GAME

This comes from Canada where it is sometimes known under the more unusual name of 'Haley Over.' It is somewhat odd in that it requires a high wall or building with a sloping roof to play over the top of. Try to choose a building where the occupants are not going to complain to the police! It is also best played with a referee, who acts as the timer when the ball is caught.

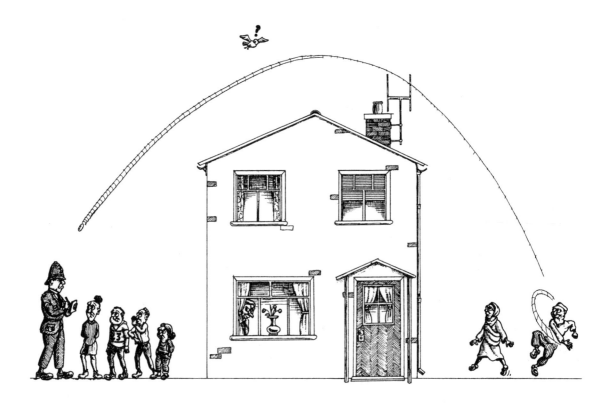

Play involves two teams of players standing on either side of the wall or building. They must not be able to see each other.

- Play begins with one player throwing the ball over the obstacle and the other team have to try and catch it. If they are successful, that player runs round the wall or building and has thirty seconds to hit players with the ball. They can accomplish this by either throwing the ball or touching players with it. Any players tagged in this way then join the tagger's side.
- If the ball is not caught, the teams take alternate turns to throw the ball back and forth across the wall.
- After a successful tagging, that team again throws the ball.
- A game ends when all the players on one side are captured.

WEIRD RACES

Youth clubs, community centres, schools and the like often hold open days, fetes and fund-raising events. Primary school children enjoy playing unusual team games and taking part in odd events. This section is for you!

Three and four legged races

In a number of towns and villages throughout the UK, not to mention in colleges and universities, sponsored runs are organised which can raise significant amounts of cash for charities and local organisations and are fun for those taking part. For a three legged race, participants choose pairs and then the left ankle is tied with a scarf, or similar, to the right ankle of their partner. In the four legged version, three people are joined together in a similar way. It is best to advise teams of three to place the smallest team member in the middle, otherwise they are destined for problems!

For children's events, the teams can either race over an agreed course or can race to various points round a field where the players drink a cup of squash at each checkpoint. For adults, the event usually involves participants drinking a half pint of beer at each of a number of pubs over an agreed route. The authors own up to having taken part in, and suffered from, a number of these silly events. We claim we only did it for charity!

Hoop Race

This can either be organised as a race or as a co-operative activity. If it is a co-operative venture you only need one hula-hoop; if it is for teams you require one hoop for each team. This game comes from the United States and is part of the New Games world collection of activities.

Either all the participants join hands forming into a single circle, or they join together in teams of roughly equal number of people. On the word "Go" the team(s) begin to thread themselves through the hoop(s). It is fun to be part of and hilarious to watch. If the circle breaks apart the hoop must be returned to the start.
A variation involves having two different sized hoops. The hoops are moved in opposite directions around the circle and where they meet causes some wonderful confusion!

Back to Back Race

Everyone joins together in pairs and then stands back to back with their partner. They join arms together and then on the command "Go," each team races over an agreed distance to a finish line. If the player's arms become unlinked then their team must go back to the start.

Scavenger Hunt

Beloved of the Scouts and Guides, the Scavenger Hunt is a form of Treasure Hunt, which can be fun and educational as well if that is the aim.

The organiser must:
• set the boundaries for how far players must travel to find the objects they are

searching for;
- give each pair the same list of objects they are seeking and provide them with a plastic bag to collect their objects in;
- set a time limit, by which players should return to the start;
- explain that items must not be damaged or stolen.

A typical list for a scavenger hunt follows, but this should be constructed depending on where the game is being played and the skills and ages of the intended players.

Items might include:
- a newspaper
- a matchbox
- a piece of string
- five different leaves
- a pinecone
- an empty bottle
- a ball of some sort.

Keep safety in mind if the pairs are going to be moving around either in an urban or rural location.

Frog or Rabbit Race

This was a very popular Victorian parlour game. You need to prepare a number of frogs or rabbits cut out of cardboard, each should be about ten inches high. About an inch from the top of each frog, punch or pierce a small hole and thread a length of string through it. The string needs to be about six feet long. The far end of the string needs to be attached firmly to something solid that is about a foot above the ground.

To start the race, all the participants have their frogs close to them and they hold the free end of the string. On "Go," all the contestants jerk the piece of string which gradually makes the frog move along towards the end of the string. The first frog to reach the end wins.

Other ideas for races

1. Team members have to carry a round object or ball balanced on paper plate across a room or over an agreed distance.
2. Players must roll a lemon with a pencil across the room.
3. Locate balloons of various colours around a room and get all the players to find balloons of their colour and blow them up.

4. Players have to eat four cream crackers and swallow them before the other players.
5. A dressing up game using a scarf, hat, coat and gloves for each team. The first player runs, puts on the items of clothing and then undresses, passing them on the next team player and so on until all the team have dressed up.
6. A leap-frog relay, with the team standing in a line and the one at the back jumping over the one in front.
7. Each player (or team) has to blow a ping pong ball across a table or smooth floor using a plastic straw.
8. Players have to move a matchbox outer between their team from nose to nose.
9. Slow bicycle race.
10. Cycle race up a steep hill, with contestants being measured to where they put down their feet.
11. Balance something like a bean bag on the head and race over an agreed course.
12. Give each team a pack of cards and a plastic bowl or tub in which they have to toss their cards. The team with the most cards in the bowl wins.
13. Soap bubble battle: players or teams alternately blow a bubble and then try to blow it over their opponent's base line.
14. British Bulldog: All the players except one, line up with their backs against a wall. On the call of "British Bulldog, one, two, three," they race to the other end of the room, and the one catcher tries to catch them. If they are picked up off the ground they join the catcher's team for the next round.
15. Prepare long winter socks with a variety of objects in them, the same for each team. The idea is then to remove the objects in a particular order, e.g. cotton reel, pen, wrapped sweet, paper clip, ping pong ball, playing card, toy car.

HOPPY CURRIE

In India we heard of hopping fights being one of the most popular childhood games and from Scotland we heard this called Hoppy Currie. The idea is simple; two contestants each stand on one foot and hop towards one another with the express intention of knocking each other off balance, thereby forcing the opponent to put their other foot down on the ground. We have seen it played with the rule that both players should keep their arms folded and then perform the function of human bumper cars. It can also be played as a knockout competition with lots of people involved. The winner is the last person left on one foot. An agreed boundary has to be set in advance, otherwise some players will use the opportunity to hop away out of sight!

WEIGH BUTTER

Being that we are still grown up bairns, Howie and Alan tried this in one of their evening watering holes before using with youngsters! The idea is for two people to link arms with each other while sitting or standing in a back-to-back position. Once they are standing in the upright position they both have to try and lift the other person's feet off the ground. Alan is a bit taller (and heavier than Howie), so the competition was hardly fair!

The game is a traditional Scottish street and playground game and originally there was a chant which went with the competition:

> Weigh butter
> Weigh cheese
> Weigh a pun' o' can'le grease.

ART ARENA GAMES

When we were both working together running practical training sessions on using games and arts and crafts for youth workers, teachers and social workers in Scotland there was a lot of interest in murals. At about the same time (1979), Don Pavey wrote, and Methuen published, his book, 'Art-based games.' It was a difficult book, but still inspirational for many workers. It offered ideas and a method of working with groups of young people for creating large scale pieces of art. This process was called an Art Arena Game, or Aag, for short.

The following offers a very much shortened and less complex introduction to the concept. Hopefully there is enough for you to feel confident to 'have a go' with any group of young people you know.

**A typical grid for an
Art Arena Game**

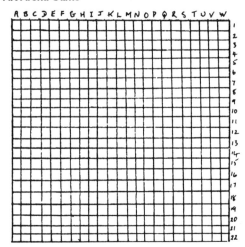

What it's all about

Don and his many colleagues were looking to offer a game model which provided fun, co-operation and an end product in the shape of a mural or large scale 'creation.' There are various stages in producing an Aag. It is a game as well as an activity because the teams are operating independently as well as co-operatively. Tensions rise and are dealt with; conflicts arise and negotiation occurs. There are no strict rules, but the process, a bit simplified, runs something like this:

- Choose a theme, something that means something for the group concerned, or will capture their imagination. It may be shapes such as crystals or circles and squares, or something closer to home like town and country.
- Prepare the surface to be painted or transformed, usually by marking out a grid on the entire area. Also prepare scaled down copies of the grid on A4 sheets of paper.
- Collect together resources for the activity: plenty of rough paper, paints, brushes, pencils, felt pens, chalks, mixing palettes, tables to work on scissors, rulers, glue(not for sniffing!) special materials such as glitter, dried beans, shiny paper etc..
- Introduce the activity to your group. Give out simple briefing notes, if necessary. If it involves some research from books, or by going out and looking at something or making sketches do this. Explain the processes:

-Aim: to produce a big picture about, for instance 'Our families.'

-How we do it? Work in teams, each with a series of sub-sections of the grid to paint. Explain that all the teams must be allowed to have their views expressed in the final painting. As Pavey's book says: "The game belongs to the players." Explain the techniques which can potentially be used in the painting: brushwork, drawing, cutting out bits from magazines and gluing etc..

-Who does what and when? In the preparation of an Aag there are various stages.

1) Players join their allocated teams. Teams are allocated a specific section of the master wall plan.

2) Everyone makes a rough design for the whole Aag.

3) In teams, the plans are discussed and the best bits are cut out and stuck down or re-drawn onto a team plan.

4) The outline of the master plan is drawn up with chalk or similar onto the team's section of the master wall. This is accomplished by using a caller who reads out grid references for each bit of drawing. A photocopier is handy on the premises to enable more than one team member to be looking at similar images.

5) A meeting takes place between all the teams to discuss how to deal with any conflicts at the overlaps and joins between sections. There may be a number of such meetings in the course of a complete game.

6) In an Aag game there can be lots of roles for players, which they can fulfil for a short time or for the whole painting period. Often there are: *planners, designers, callers, painters and possibly negotiators to deal with other teams.*

7) The activity takes place with callers directing painters, and designers making refinements to the detailed plans, and negotiators dealing with disputed art territory. Pavey refers to it as, "A balance between freedom and control."

8) Final conference to evaluate the end creation. This can be formalised with marking the game, looking at:
- the overall work
- individual contributions
- teamwork
- how much fun?
- how far does it reflect the original aim?

Improvise

We've already said that it is not a game with one set structure or set of rules. It takes a fair amount of time planning and preparing and can take between two and five hours to finish. This can sometimes be accommodated in one session, but it may need to take place at a series of meetings. The game should fit the group members, not the other way round, so as the organiser, try to choose subjects which are stimulating and relevant.

One of our colleagues, Chris Archer, working in Borders Region of Scotland built a framework onto which each Aag project could be fixed while it was in preparation. Some of the murals his youth groups created were hung in the local junior library when completed. We'll finish with a quote from Chris about his use of Art Arena Games: *"Plan everything carefully, and give the team an opportunity to develop games for themselves, but not to be disappointed if things flounder. Be alive to this possibility and have plenty of ideas to help the children get to grips with the venture. Then, sooner or later, this will be repaid as they and the game 'takes off.' Remember, the aim is fun for all........a successful Art Arena Game not only looks good, but it feels good."*

KICK THE CAN

Early in this century and even between the two World Wars, entertainment for children mostly took place in the streets. Kick the Can is a game we have heard mentioned from both Scottish and Welsh friends. There is no single set of rules, but two versions we have heard described could still be played today without anything more elaborate than a reasonably substantial can with both ends removed. A used treacle tin was one of the favourites in the 30s and 40s.

Version One

This version is basically a game of hide and seek. The searcher would kick the can as far they could from a starting point and then run after it. While they were doing this, everyone else involved in the game went and hid. They had as long as it took the searcher to reach the can and kick it back to its starting point. From then on the game is one of hide-and-seek.

Version Two

The was also known as Kick the Can or 'Block the Can', and involved no hiding. It was sometimes played as an individual game, sometimes as a team game. To start with the first player would kick the can from a starting point which was marked in some way on the ground. Then the can would be passed around between the players with each taking a turn to try and kick the can back to its original starting place.

FRENCH CRICKET

We played this a lot when we were school kids, and have introduced it successfully to playschemes and recreation events. Even though it is called 'French' cricket, we have no idea about its true origins. It is very simple and because it is fast and less formal than the real game of cricket, it is good for playing with younger groups and mixed gender groups.

All you require is a cricket bat and a tennis ball. It can be played by anything between two and about a dozen players.

- One player goes into bat first. Their own legs and feet (shoes) below the knees are their wicket. They must keep their legs firmly together and try to guard their wicket.
- One of the fielding/bowling side throws the ball underarm towards the batter's legs. If the batter hits it they may move their legs. If the batter misses, they must stay exactly where they are.

- The next bowl is taken from the point where a fielder stops the earlier bowl. This can mean that the batter is holding the bat round behind their legs. It is all part of the fun!
- A player is out if they are caught, or bowled, with the ball touching any part of the batter's legs or feet.
- There is no method of scoring, unless each 'hit' is scored as one run, and a boundary is awarded four or six runs.
- Usually, the successful bowler or catcher takes over batting when they gain a wicket.

GREEK-BALL

We cannot guarantee that this game is Greek, but we think it may have originated somewhere there. It is a good activity game, which combines a relay race with a ball game. You need about four a side to play and everyone needs to be able to run, so it is not suitable for people with disabilities.

To play you need a football, or similar, and a court marked out into four squares, as in the diagram:

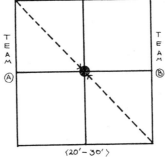

The two teams line up facing one another, and the ball is placed right in the middle of the intersection. The first person acting as a runner for each team is positioned in the opposite corner of the square pitch. Ideally, you need an umpire who can blow a whistle or call 'go.' At this signal the runner from each team races from their corner and tries to gain possession of the ball. Whoever is successful then tries to throw the ball over the heads of the opposing players. Defending players are not allowed to enter into the playing square, but can try to catch or intercept the ball from outside.

If the ball goes past the defending team, the thrower's team wins a point, and the process is repeated with two new runners, one from each team. If the defending team stops their opponents from scoring they can throw the ball to their player in the middle who can attempt, from the centre point, to try and throw the ball over the other team's heads.

The size of the playing area should be varied to suit the ages and abilities of the players. Somewhere in the range twenty to thirty fee square seems to work well. It is a game well suited to many indoor games halls as well as for playing field or beach. It is best to set a time limit of about twenty minutes for the duration of a game.

PULLING THE ROD

Also known as 'Pulling the Baton,' this is an old Shetland game (as far as we know). It is a bit like 'Weigh the Butter' described elsewhere in this section. It is another game for two contestants. To play you need a stout stick about two foot long. Both players sit on the ground with their knees drawn up towards their chests. They both then grip the stick tightly with the soles of their shoes pressed firmly together. The aim is pull the opponent up out of their seated position so that they are standing.

THREE WAY TUG OF WAR

This is an interesting variation on the more normal tug of war which requires two teams and a single rope. In this version three players can have an amusing tug of war competition by joining a rope together into a continuous circle. The players then form the rope into a triangular shape and on the command, "Go" they each try and pull their two contestants towards them. As in regular tug of war, it is useful to have a mark on the ground to show who has pulled whom the furthest.

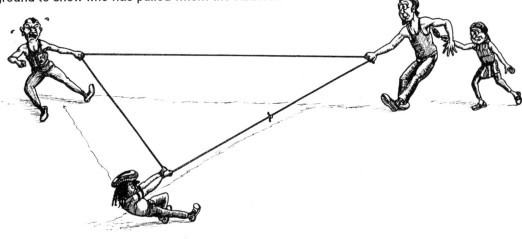

A **further variation** can involve fixing permanent rope tails to the tip of each triangle. This then allows three teams to pull on their rope, once again trying to pull both the opposition teams towards them.

COIN THROWING

Coin throwing games, and games involving the throwing or flicking of playing cards and cigarette cards have been popular in a number of countries. In each of these games, they were originally used for gambling, so the easiest way to play with young people and remove the gambling element is to each start off with the same number of coins, which are returned to their owners after use!

Penny on the drum

This an Anglicisation of a French game much beloved by Napoleon's soldiers. Any number can take part. The idea was to have soldiers throw a small value coin (probably one centime, originally) onto a drum. You can use a tray instead. If a coin lands with the same side upwards and overlaps another coin, the player wins that coin. If that coin was overlapping other coins, these are won as well. An end game to decide who wins all the remaining coins on the drum is to place a small silver coin, say our five pence, on the drum and then the first player to cover the coin, or partially cover it, wins all the remaining coins.

Brother Jonathan

This is an eighteenth century coin tossing game from North America. It involves chalking a board out on the ground and a throwing line, behind which the players have to stand. The segments of the board each have a score value and coins only score if they are inside of the lines. The smallest sections have the highest scores. Play continues with each player taking alternate throws. The game ends when one player reaches a predetermined total score, or the winner is the player with highest score at the end of an agreed number of throws.

Bottle toss

On a number of occasions we have used a bottle toss to successfully raise funds for youth clubs we have been running. The idea is to place a bottle in the middle of a large-ish floor space and then invite people to toss or roll coins towards the bottle with the intention of getting their coin closest to the bottle, ideally touching it. Usually, since it is a fund-raising game, the person with the closest coin wins the bottle after an agreed length of time. When organising this game it is best to have a referee keeping an eye on the proceedings, otherwise you may find yourself with disputes over who-threw-which-coin.

JEU DE BOULES (or Pétanque)

The impulse to throw a pebble or roll a round stone along the ground has been with man since earliest civilisation. Ancient Egyptian vases show young men propelling balls along the ground in some sort of competition - and that was 4,000 years ago! In the UK, the bowling green at Southampton has been in continuous use since 1299. But that is Lawn bowls, or in the north of England, Crown green bowls, played on an uneven rink. Neither game is regarded as a game which children play. However, the French game of Boules, also known as Pétanque is gradually becoming a popular beach and back-garden game.

A set of boules or bocce (the Italian version of the same game) are essentially similar. They are metal balls of about three and a half inches diameter and weigh about one and a half pounds. In the two-player game, each player uses three or four boules; with teams of two, each player uses three boules. Players usually mark their own boules or bocce with distinguishing marks. For each game a small, wooden jack called the *cochonnet* is thrown up the rink and must land between the bowling line and boundary line.

In the UK, sets of weighted plastic boules are cheaply available from many toy and sports shops. They are not as much fun to play with, but are perhaps best for youth groups who might be tempted to use the metal boule as an offensive weapon!

To play:

The Rink: Unlike Lawn bowls, boules can be played on just about any surface, but it is most usually played in France on a strip of hard gravel or sand about 80 or 90 feet long and 10 feet wide. Alan visited the Languedoc region of France recently, and there in Lavaur saw about thirty men and children playing boules on the site of one of the most vicious massacres of the Albigensian Crusade, where over 400 men and women were burned for heresy and the first Lady of the town was bricked up alive in the well, exactly underneath the present boules court!

The rink is marked up with a boundary and bowling line at each end.

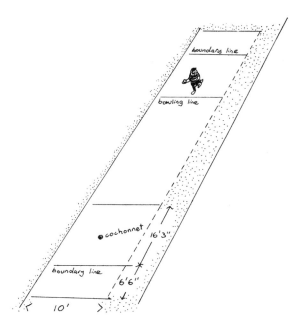

Play begins: The cochonnet is thrown up to the other end of the rink, then one player called the *bouliste,* can either throw the boule (*portée*) through the air or roll it (*boule pointée*) towards the cochonnet. Players must not cross the bowling line until after the boule has landed.

The first player only throws one boule, then the next player throws their boules until they get the closest boule to the cochonnet, referred to as *best boule.* This marks the end of their turn. Play continues in this way until all of the boules have been thrown.

Scoring: Each boule closer to the cochonnet than the opponent's best boule scores one point. A measuring rod, twenty inches long, called a *baguette* is used to measure the distance between boules and the cochonnet. After adding up the score, players change ends and the player/team which won the last end throws up the cochonnet for the new game, and throws the first boule. A game usually lasts for either 13 or 15 points.

WORLD OF RELATIONSHIP GAMES

Relationship Games
   Introduction....96
About Me....99
Pairs....99
Picture Pairs....100
Characteristics....101
Wordles....101
Guggenheim....102
Squeeze the Knee....104
Blind Run....105
Problems....105
Connections....106
Mind Game....107
All Stand...108
Getting to Know You....108
Personal Shields....109
Adverts....110
Mime Challenge....110
Affirmation Rounds....111
Pack your Bag....112
Five of the Best....113
Guess my Name....113
Messages....114
Pass the Squeeze -
   variation....115
Off your chest....116
Statements....117
Your Number's up....119
Tell me True....120
Likes and Dislikes....120
Chinese Whispers....121
Birthday Present....122
Active Listening....122

Sex Roles....123
Catch Me if You Can...124
Human Train....125
Comments....126
Speakeasy....127
Escape....128
Demo....129
Improvise....130
Rivers....130
Romania/Bulgaria....131
Triple Names....132
Partisan....132
What's your Name -
   Lemonade!....133
Cold, Warm, Hot....134
Frankenstein....134
Cat and Mouse....135
Harlem Shuffle....136
Back Dance....136

RELATIONSHIP GAMES - INTRODUCTION

We would advise spending time planning any games session, whether it be in the classroom, home or youth club. In using relationship games, due to the kind of feedback and emotional response some of these techniques are designed to produce, it is important to prepare **appropriate** games and anticipate **potential reactions.**

In our previous publication, the *New Youth Games Book* we included a thorough introduction to the use of relationship games, and we recommend this to you. Those of you who find relationship games interesting or useful will certainly want to get hold of a copy - taken together, the relationship games sections in both books provide comprehensive coverage of this fascinating area. Over 120 different techniques are included, and what's more, there is no repetition of games between the two books!

In this brief introduction we will cover the main factors involved in using this type of game, activity or sequence. Relationship games are used for three main purposes:

- to help groups of people get to know one another better and more quickly than would otherwise be the case;
- to help groups explore difficult issues in a positive way;
- to enable individuals to develop skills, confidence and trust.

There are several categories of relationship game - we group these into two main sections, 'Icebreakers' and the 'Heavy End,' to reflect their two main purposes.

Icebreakers

These are techniques designed to help groups get to know one another. They include games and techniques which help new groups to remember one another's names quickly and to share basic information about each other and our likes, dislikes etc.. Icebreakers also include the 'trust games' category, designed to encourage group members to trust and depend on one another.

Typically, these are physical techniques which also help to reduce anxieties about physical contact, particularly between the sexes. These physical trust games **always** demand the presence of one or more adult helpers to make sure that the rules are followed and that no-one comes to any harm. They also help young people to overcome embarrassment and encourage active participation.

Some icebreakers, e.g. of the 'name game' type are useful in the early stages of a new group when there is a need for people to learn names quickly. Of course, if your group is meeting with another group they do not know at a later stage (or e.g. holding a party with invited guests), then name games can be very useful. Other icebreakers can be used at any stage in

a group's development to re-inforce the learning already achieved, or simply because the group enjoys playing them. Physical trust games are a good example - it is always useful to re-inforce group members' trust in one another, and young people tend to enjoy these techniques.

The Heavy End

These techniques should only be used with a group once trust has been established. They are not suitable for the early stages of a new group, although they can be used straight away with groups, e.g. a family group, where members already know one another well. Generally, we would always suggest using a few icebreakers immediately before using 'heavy end' techniques as this helps get the group into a game playing frame of mind, and also serves to re-inforce group cohesion.

'Heavy end' games usually involve disclosure (telling people things about yourself that you might not normally share) or risk-taking (trying out things you haven't done before, e.g. miming or acting). Relationship games in general, and 'heavy end' games in particular, are very powerful mechanisms for increasing individuals' self-esteem. They tend to be used extensively by youth social workers with groups of young people who have experienced a range of difficulties in their lives.

'Heavy end' games need to be used sensitively - in most cases it is a good idea to have a 'let out' rule so that a participant need not take their turn, or indeed participate in a particular game, if they feel threatened. Our experience is that this kind of rule is rarely abused. As far as possible, you need to match the game to the group's stage of development - some can be very challenging and are only suitable for groups where trust has been well established and individuals are used to taking risks with one another.

Other issues

It is important when using relationship games that adults in the group participate in playing them as well; otherwise, the young people may be distrustful and less inclined to participate themselves. This is crucial with games which pose a threat or challenge - also, it is not a good idea for adult helpers in a group to use a 'let out' rule.

Relationship games need to be introduced confidently, by an adult in the first instance, unless you happen to have a young person in your group who is already well acquainted with a particular technique. It can be very useful for the adult helpers to have a 'dry run' on their own with games they are unfamiliar with - in this way you can usually pick up on any idiosyncrasies in the game, unusual rules etc.. In order to play some of the games, you may need to get together with other adults to make up the numbers. We have found it useful, when doing this kind of 'dry run,' to rôle play particular young people in our groups - this gives a really good feel for how some individuals are likely to react to a particular game.

Many relationship games benefit from what we call 'de-briefing' - this offers the group the opportunity to talk about how they felt while playing the game; particular lessons learned; ideas for variations of the game, and so on. With techniques which involve young people taking up particular rôles, we talk about 'de-rôling,' where you allow individuals a few minutes to remind themselves that they are no longer play-acting someone else but are back in the real world once more.

In the *New Youth Games Book* we used separate sections for 'icebreakers' and 'heavy end' techniques. We have not done so in this chapter, although we have given advice in the text as to a game's suitability for 'introductory' or 'advanced' groups.

ABOUT ME

This is a short introductory game which can be useful in new groups and for breaking the ice. To start the sequence off, organise all the group members into pairs and brief them, saying that they should each say two things about themselves. It is useful to offer a couple of examples such as:

> *The first thing I do in the morning when I get up is to go for a pee.*
> *I catch a bus to go to school.*

The other member of the pair then offers two statements about themselves. Then, partners switch round and repeat the sequence with somebody different. This continues until everyone has met all the other members of the group.

Because it takes place in lots of pairs, it gives everyone a relatively non-threatening opportunity to say something about themselves and learn something about other people. It can be helpful if the organiser controls the changeover of the pairs, either by calling out, "Change partners" or by some other signal.

PAIRS

Group leaders will often want to split a large group into pairs; here are a couple of ways to do it which are great fun - especially with new groups. The first technique originates in the States, and appears as 'Hog Call' in the literature - apparently because North American farmers used to gather their cattle with an ear-splitting howl reminiscent of a hog on a hot tin roof.

This exercise demands plenty of space and should be played outdoors, or in a large games hall. First of all, split your large group into two facing lines; you can make the 'line-up' more interesting by asking folk to line up by age, the month in which their birthdays fall etc.. Now ask folk to introduce themselves to the person opposite (i.e. in the other line) by shaking hands, swapping names, etc..Each pair should now choose for themselves a matching set of words, e.g. bread-jam, mickey-mouse, dog-bone etc.. Each person in a pair should choose *one* of their words as their own. Ask each pair to announce their selection - the group should be able to enjoy one or two laughs from the weirder selections! Gently rule out any duplicates and ask these pairs to choose again.

Now ask each line to move to opposite ends of the games hall, field etc. - make sure they mix themselves up on the way, so that they are no longer facing their original partner. Explain to the group that they will now be blindfolded (or asked to keep their eyes firmly shut) and asked to mill around, shouting their partner's word until they can find one another - by voice and touch alone!

You will need to cover the safety aspects by teaching the 'bumpers up' position, i.e. folk should hold their arms out in front of them with palms facing forward - this minimises the physical risk as people bump into one another (which they are meant to do - this is half the fun!). You must also have a few responsible helpers spread about the playing area to prevent people from bumping into walls or other obstructions (trees etc. if you are playing outdoors). Be sure to brief the group that they will be well looked out for while they are blindfold - apart from being great fun this is a trust exercise and should be introduced as such with all the appropriate safeguards.

This technique creates a nice cacophony of sounds, particularly indoors - if the noise level is likely to be a problem, just get folk to whisper instead, as its just as much fun! Once someone has found their partner, they can move off together to a quieter area and introduce one another a bit more fully by finding out some information about one another, e.g. favourite food, pop star etc.. Once everyone has found their partner you can form the group into a seated circle and invite someone to introduce their partner as fully as possible - the partner reciprocates and then nominates someone else to introduce their own partner.

PICTURE PAIRS

This works well with large groups and doesn't require the same kind of space as 'Hog Call.' It doesn't need to be used exclusively with a new group and is particularly nice to use in a 'party' environment when you want people to pair up at random.

All you need as preparation for this technique is one picture (from a newspaper or colour magazine) for each pair you want to create; so if you have a group of twenty, you'll need ten pictures. Each picture should be cut up 'jigsaw fashion' to form two halves. Now mix up all the pictures, put them in a hat or simlar container, and invite each person to choose one.

Players must now mill around trying to find the missing half of their picture, and thus their partner for the next event you have in mind!

CHARACTERISTICS

This is a useful activity to encourage the group to think about the characteristics of individuals within it. You will need a large piece of paper, e.g. several flipchart sheets stapled together, and a marker pen for each person in the group.

In the middle of the paper, draw a large circle to represent the group. Have the group sit or stand around the piece of paper and invite them to think for a minute or two about individual characteristics which would be helpful to the group as a whole. Now ask people to pick up a pen and write one or two words *inside* the circle which represent how they would like to see group members work together (e.g. helpful, caring, responsible etc.).

Now allow the group a minute or two to think about individual characteristics which are unhelpful to the group - and this time write them on the *outside* of the circle (e.g. name-calling, put-downs etc.).

Once this process is complete, invite people to explain what they mean by their particular words. This is so that everyone has a common understanding of what is meant, since individuals may use their words with a slightly different nuance.

This is a useful activity to use as part of the debriefing process at the end of a session - particularly so because the young people themselves have identified their positives and negatives. The process also allows people to make positive or negative comments about one another in an indirect, and therefore non-threatening way. The adult leader should encourage discussion of the characteristics raised, in particular checking that they make sense as positives or negatives. This is a really excellent way in to discussing the effects that individual characteristics and behaviours can have on the group process generally.

Of course, the characteristics identified can easily form the basis of a set of group rules as the characteristics identified are essentially a set of behaviours. Indeed the group may want to keep their set of 'characteristics' as a reminder of agreed group norms.

WORDLES

These are word puzzles which have been prepared on pieces of card in advance. They are a new name for an old series of recreations often called by such names as 'enigmas, transpositions, anagrams and rebuses.' The name 'Wordles' has been applied to them by Karl Rohnke in his book, 'Silver Bullets' (Kendall Hunt/Project Adventure, 1984).

The idea is to set up lots of short word puzzles, each written out on separate cards. The game can be organised as a co-operative challenge for one small group, or with two or more equal-sized groups competing. The cards are distributed with an even number going to each group, or at least one for each member of a single group. Part of the challenge for the organiser is to create enough cards to enable them to provide words and puzzles which can provide fun and an appropriate level of difficulty for different abilities.

As each Wordle card is solved, the team can move on to the next problem, but according to Karl's rules, a team should struggle on for two minutes on any card, the answer to which is proving elusive. If it is a team game, the winning team is the first to finish their batch of cards. If there is just one group, it is purely a group challenge and affords a good opportunity for co-operation and teamwork.

Below we provide a variety of potential Wordles. As group members get used to the sequence, it is fun to get them making up their own Wordle challenges.

1. NOTLOB

2. NOON LAZY

3. NME NMG NME SURROUND NE NME NME NME

4. PROMISES

5. EZ

6. ESCORT

7. BLIND3

8. CAT in SCHOOLING

9. Animal in Newspaper

10.

11. SGEG

12. CYCLE CYCLE CYCLE

13. NO DO LON

14. YOUR PaANNTTsS

15. Small lamb in Brewery

16. BAN ANA

17. STAND

18. SIDE SIDE

19. BJOKACX

20. A

Wordle Answers

1. Bolton
2. Lazy afternoon
3. Surrounded by enemies
4. Broken promises
5. Easy
6. Corset
7. Mice
8. Education
9. Ape
10. Bridge over troubled water
11. Scrambled eggs
12. Tri-cycle
13. London
14. Ants in your pants
15. Ewe
16. Banana split
17. I understand
18. Side by side
19. Jack in the Box
20. Matinee

GUGGENHEIM

We included this word game in our earliest *Youth Games Book* and then our typesetter or paste-up artist lost it somewhere en route to a later edition and we forgot about it. More recently it has resurfaced as the commercial game, 'Scattergories,' but you can learn how to play it for free!

This is a good game and one which is very popular with children as soon as they are confident enough to write. It originated in America, where it seems to be related in some way to the Guggenheims, who were a Philadelphian mining family. Its appearance in games books coincided with the invention of the crossword puzzle in about 1913.

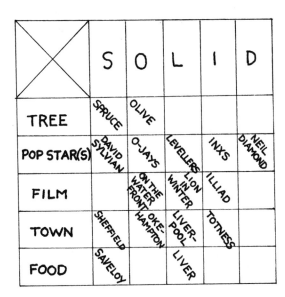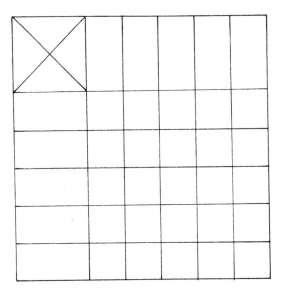

To play each player requires a paper and pen or pencil and a timing device: egg-timer or stop watch. Each player needs to draw up a grid as above, or you can photocopy the blank one for handing out to players.

- First, decide on how many categories you are going to include. With younger groups we usually use five, but for older groups up to twelve is fine.
- Then, decide on how long to allow for each game. If you try one game out with your group using a five minute time-limit, you'll quickly be able to assess the optimum time to suit the ability levels of your players.
- The games organiser calls out five (or however many) categories for the players. Try to choose categories which are appropriate to the group. These are written in to the boxes in the left hand column. For instance, for young people, the following are suitable:

  boys' names; girls' names; animals; types of food; TV programmes; film stars; pop groups; names of towns; rivers; authors; politicians; birds; trees; types of vehicle.

- One of the players should be invited to choose a five letter word with no double letters, such as S-O-L-I-D, which everyone writes in the five boxes across the top of the grid. The organiser calls, "Go" and everyone tries to fill in the categories using words beginning with the five letters across the top (see the example).
- Players should be urged to seek out unusual words since these may score more.
- On the call of "Time" everyone stops writing.
- Scoring rules vary, but we suggest awarding one point for every correct word, with one bonus point for words which no-one else has.

Guggenheim is a fast and enjoyable game, but may be too difficult for some young people with a limited vocabulary.

SQUEEZE THE KNEE

This variation of 'Pass the Squeeze' (New Youth Games Book) is played in Russia, we believe. It is suitable for all sizes of group, but is most fun with a largish group of 15-30 people.

Players should be sitting close together in a circle - on chairs or cross-legged on the floor. Each person puts their hands on the knees of the people on either side of them - hence the need for people to be sitting cosily next to one another. This can create quite a tangle, so make sure that folk realise that their right hand should be on the left knee of the person to their right and that their left hand should be on the right knee of the person on their left. Confused? You will be once you start playing!

One person should be nominated to start the sequence off - they must decide which way the squeeze will go. Obviously, if they decide to send it to the right they should use their right hand to squeeze the left knee of the person on their right - this *should* be dead easy as their right hand should already be resting on the appropriate left knee! The person whose knee has been squeezed then passes the squeeze on in the same direction.

Be sure to allow only gentle squeezes of the knee as these bits of the anatomy can be quite sensitive if handled roughly. Unlike Pass the Squeeze this is not a guessing game but a group challenge, so to begin with see if the group can 'squeeze the knee' all the way round the circle without making a mistake. This is easier said than done as it can be quite difficult to work out which hand to use.

Once this has been achieved you may want to challenge the group to complete the sequence in a specified time - and following this, as fast as possible. This is a fun sequence involving close proximity and physical contact, so you may want to use it in a sequence of other physical contact games or as a prelude to physical trust games. Allow 10-20 minutes depending on the size of your group.

NEWS OF THE YEAR

With this technique you are inviting individuals to think about a piece of news which has had a significant effect on them. Ideally, you want people to think of an item of media news, but 'personal' news, e.g. the birth of a brother or sister, can also be included if you wish (as many young people are not terrifically affected by media events!).

This works best when used with a small group. Sitting in a circle, invite the group to cast their minds back over the past year to identify a piece of news which has had a significant effect on them. This could be, for example: a person's football team winning an important match; the resignation of the government (fat chance!) or the death of a favourite pop star.

Now invite group members in turn to share their 'news of the year' with the others. Allow time for questions and discussion after each news item, so that the group builds an awareness of the ways in which events can affect people.

Bear in mind when using the technique in this kind of open-ended way that you can easily get 'heavy' news items being introduced, e.g. the death of a relative. If you are not working with a well established group, it is best to limit folk to 'good news' items only.

This technique can be used as a useful way into discussions about the media and how we are all affected by it.

BLIND RUN

As this is a potentially risky trust sequence, it should only be used with a well established group which is well versed in trust techniques. 'Blind Run' needs to be played in a games hall or similar, where there are no obstructions and plenty of space.

First of all brief your 'catchers' - this should comprise the whole group bar the person who has volunteered first for the 'Blind Run.' Most of the catchers should form two lines, a few feet apart, near the back wall of your games hall; they should have their backs to the wall. From the other end of the hall the volunteer is going to jog blindfold (or with eyes tight shut) towards the two lines. The volunteer should use the 'bumpers up' position - arms outstretched with palms facing forwards.

The job of the catchers is self-evident - prevent the volunteer smashing into the wall. The second line is a fail safe and the catching team should aim to stop the runner at the first line. As you can become quite disorientated when blindfold, you will need to have some catchers standing by the side walls about three quarters if the way down the hall to catch any runners who are wildly off course. Due to the risk element with 'Blind Run,' don't allow *any* fooling around on the part of the catchers.

This is an excellent technique for building high levels of trust - we find that group members are keen to discuss their feelings after the exercise, e.g. how much 'bottle' it takes to do it.

PROBLEMS

Use this technique with smallish groups who know one another fairly well. In advance you will need to prepare cards with one problem on each card, for example:

- skips school
- can't play pool to save their life
- thinks people are getting at them
- has a tough time at home.

Create 'doublers' of each card and make sure to include cards which are suitable for adults. Clearly you can personalise these cards to suit your group members, but be sure to avoid issues which are confidential, or only known by adults in the group.

Now stick these cards on a wall with blu-tac and on the opposite wall put up cards with the names of group members, including adults. Now ask group members to choose problems that they think belong to them, and ask them to put the problems under their own name. Ask the group to look at each other's selections and then encourage a discussion on why particular cards were chosen.

A more difficult variation is to use good points about yourself, rather than problems. Finally, at a later stage in the group you can ask them to select the problems and good points that they think others have - in this way you invite feedback on how individuals are viewed in the group and the community.

CONNECTIONS

We have found this to be a good group game. We suspect that there are almost as many variations as there are potential players. It is a derivation of the 'Word Association' game we described in the *New Youth Games Book*. We have used the sequence in both formal and informal group situations and in travel situations where the game can help to relieve boredom. We used it mostly as a non-competitive sequence, allowing the group to take as long or as short a time to try and reach the connected word.

The idea is to make up sets of odd words. These may be best prepared in advance on cards; for instance:

COD & BOOK

As in 'Word Association,' it is a good idea to play the game fast, perhaps using a three clap-space sequence, so, in this example it might proceed round a group:

> "Cod" *clap - clap - clap*
> "Fish" *clap - clap - clap*
> "Sea" *clap - clap - clap*
> "Land" *clap - clap - clap*
> "Land's End" *clap - clap - clap*
> "Book end" *clap - clap - clap*
> "Book" *clap - clap - clap*

It may seem a bit convoluted, but it is good fun and it makes for a good co-operative exercise. We usually allow about ten minutes to quarter of an hour for this sequence.

It can also be used as a competitive sequence (or even a one-player game) with each player trying to see how few connections are necessary to link together the starting and finishing words.

Try to make your word pairs random and definitely 'unconnected.' Suggestions include:
BALL & CRAYON
CARROT & BOTTLE OF WINE
DOG & SUN
GUITAR & SHOE

MIND GAME

This fascinating technique was shown to us by John McWhirter, who hails from Glasgow. 'Mind Game' can be classed as American, as it illustrates one of the many interesting concepts to come out of 'NLP' - otherwise known as (wait for it!) Neuro-Linguistic Programming. No, it doesn't involve wiring your favourite computer up directly to the old brain cells; but it does offer us some amazing insights into the way our minds work (or sometimes don't!).

We've found that this activity works best with a small group - it can be used with larger groups as a 'spectator' event, as long as the group is well enough established to suspend their disbelief about what they are about to witness.

Two people are needed to demonstrate the technique, and first time round it is best if the adult facilitator takes the lead role. As far as equipment goes, you will need a chair - ideally without armrests.

Mind Game demonstrates, in a very simple way, the power of mind over matter. The 'matter' in this case is your volunteer, who should be asked to sit (not slouch!) in the chair. You should face the volunteer, and talk directly to them, persuading them that they are feeling absolutely lousy; they have just had one of the worst days of their life and are feeling completely lethargic and lacking in energy; have broken up with their partner, and to cap it all - despite spending a large fortune - haven't won a red cent on the National Lottery!

Now stand behind your volunteer, place your hands lightly on their shoulders - with just enough pressure to create slight resistance as they try to get out of the chair - and ask them to stand up. With most people, you will find that they have some difficulty in actually raising themselves up from the chair.

The fact is that the pressure you exerted on their shoulders was no way enough to stop them standing up - the only other factor involved was their brain cells, which obviously fell for the suggestions you made about their state of mind.

Now repeat the activity with the same volunteer, but this time you will suggest that they are happy, feeling great and full of energy. No prizes for guessing what happens when they try to stand up this time. Other members of the group can now be invited to try the activity.

Mind Game is a useful discussion leader with a small group - it can lead you straight into discussion about the way that we *think* affects in a very direct way how we *feel* and *what we do*. Particularly with young people who tend to experience lack of self esteem this can be a real eye opener and a graphic demonstration of the power of positive thinking.

ALL STAND

This is a pairs sequence and can be used with two people, or two hundred and two. 'All Stand' is very similar to 'Pulling the Rod' which is included in Chapter 3 in this book. It is best played outdoors, or on mats or a carpet inside. Do not play 'All Stand' on a hard or slippy surface as there is the possibility of people falling and hitting their heads.

This should be introduced as a trust sequence and should be used with other similar techniques. First of all ask players to team up with someone of the same size and physical build. The pairs should then sit down on the ground or floor surface facing one another and with the soles of their shoes pressed firmly against their partners. The final stage is for pairs to reach out and grasp each others hands, and then pull as hard as they can so that they pull each other up into a standing position.

This is not a particularly easy exercise - both strength and determination are needed - so plenty of encouragement is the order of the day.

Once your group has mastered this you can encourage groups of between six and eight to try it. Have them sit in a tight circle with feet touching in the middle - then grasp hands and pull.

As with any trust sequence, don't forget the safety brief at the beginning, stressing that each person is totally reliant on their partner not to let go suddenly.

GETTING TO KNOW YOU

This is a useful activity to use in the early stages of a new group when people are still getting to know one another. You will need photocopies of a list similar to the one below - one for each person. Obviously you can tailor these pro-formas to suit particular groups you are working with. You have more flexibility with this technique if you use it with groups of more than twelve.

Explain to the group that doing this activity will help them discover a few things about one another - the aim is to get a signature against each of the items. To get their signatures they have to mingle with the rest of the group until they find someone who matches each item. Challenge the group to get a *different* signature for each item if at all possible.

Has lived in the same house all their life ....

Has lived in more than three different houses ....

Had cornflakes for breakfast ....

Goes camping in the summer ....

Likes curries ....

Has their own pet ....

Can swim 10 lengths ....

Can play a penny whistle ....

Can play a guitar ....

Watches more than 3 soap operas a week ....

Can cook a meal ....

Likes bright clothes ....

Wears an earring ....

Belongs to a youth club ....

Have travelled abroad ....

Sometimes wear glasses ....

Have a brother or a sister ....

PERSONAL SHIELDS

We think we filched this from our own 'Youth Arts & Crafts Book', which we hope will see the light of day again - sometime before the next millennium! Whether these 'Personal Shields' or 'Coats of Arms' are drawn, painted or crafted from wood, they have proved to be immensely popular with all ages. Boys in particular take to them if they are immersed in the nuances of football heraldry.

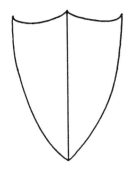 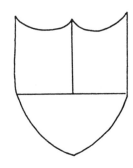

The challenge to individuals is to design their own unique 'Personal Shield'. If possible, offer them some visual examples, e.g. coat of arms of their own town, city or school. It should include elements of their own lives e.g. skateboarding, dominoes, cycling etc..

ADVERTS

This technique works best with a group of eight to ten young people who know each other reasonably well. You will need some cards prepared with a group member's name on each one. Each person should select a card with someone else's name on it.

Now explain that the task is to write an appropriate personal advert for that person, in order to 'sell' their qualities and personality to e.g. a prospective employer. Allow the group 5-10 minutes to write their adverts, then collect them in and mix them up well. The adverts should now be read out, *without* the person's name being revealed. The group should be invited to guess both the name of the person being advertised and the name of the person who wrote the advert.

MIME CHALLENGE

Similar in many respects to 'Chinese Whispers,' this mime activity is great fun to play with small groups and can be used 'spectator style' with larger groups. You will need five or six volunteers, who could be sitting together as part of a larger group or 'out at the front.'

Starting at one end of the group of six, the first person is asked to *think of* an everyday activity (e.g. having a wash, making a sandwich, getting up and going to school) and to begin to mime it. So in the example of 'getting up and going to school' the first person might mime waking up and pulling on some clothes. The second person tries to identify the mime (without disclosing it to the group) and goes on to mime the next stage - in this case, having a wash perhaps. Number three might mime having breakfast while four mimes leaving the house and waiting at the bus-stop. Number five could mime getting on the bus and sitting chatting with some pals, with six getting off the bus and running in to school to sit at their desk.

This mime sequence can be quite a challenge for some young people, while others will relish the gaming aspects. It is likely that perfect rounds will be few and far between and great fun can be had when the group realise that they began by making sandwiches and ended up in the swimming pool!

If you choose to develop the activity into a discussion you will want to tease out similar communication issues as in 'Chinese Whispers,' this time concentrating perhaps on the importance of having the right *kind* and *quality* of information, in order to make accurate deductions; i.e., not only does the mime a person does have to *be* accurate (kind of information), it has to be *seen to be* accurate (quality of information) by the people you are communicating with.

AFFIRMATION ROUNDS

These are particularly powerful when used at the end of sessions where there has been real development in trust and friendship among group members. Everyone should be sitting comfortably in a circle. The group leader nominates each person in turn to receive statements of affirmation from members of the group. These are **positive** statements.

Statements should be limited to two or three about each person, especially in a large group. With this kind of 'disclosure' exercise the adult members may have to make the first few statements. They could be along the lines of: *'Janey always makes people laugh,' 'I think she is always honest when asked her opinion about something.'*

Variations

As a prelude to using affirmation rounds in this powerful, personal way, they can be used to seek positive comments about the *session* rather than an individual. Simply invite each person to state one or two good things that happened to them, or which they enjoyed during the activities/session etc..

Of course you can also use rounds such as this to highlight some of the tensions that are around for group members. This 'raises the anti' considerably and requires both firmness and sensitivity on the part of the group leader. However, at a fairly safe level, there can be gains for the group if you allow individuals to comment (if they wish, and *after* offering some positives) on something negative that happened during the session.

As leader, you will have to decide in advance whether you will invite the group to discuss or do anything about the issues raised - or whether the issues are simply to be offered to the group without any discussion.

PACK YOUR BAG

This technique can be used with up to twenty players, who should know one another fairly well. You will need some paper and pens and should explain to the group that this game involves someone packing a bag for a holiday. Now ask for the first volunteer who wishes to take a holiday - this person should be asked to leave the room.

The other players now pack an imaginary suitcase for the volunteer. The case should be packed with objects or qualities which the volunteer is known to possess, but also with things which the group *would like* the volunteer to have. Each player should decide on one thing to go in the case - you could end up with things like 'nice sunshine, an even temper, some smart clothes,' etc..

Once the list has been drawn up the volunteer is invited back into the room and asked to guess who packed which object or quality.

This technique is interesting in that it ascertains how group members see one another *and* how they *think* they are seen.

FIVE OF THE BEST

This technique is designed to encourage people to think positively about themselves. It is only suitable for small groups of up to eight or ten. The group should have built up some basic trust before using this sequence, so it is best to avoid it in the first few sessions of a new group.

Everyone should be seated for this exercise and should be equipped with paper and pencil. As a preamble, explain to the group that everyone has good points, whether this is something they are good at doing, the way they feel about themselves, or their attitudes to people.

Now invite group members to write down 'five of the best' - five things that can be seen as good points - together with examples of these points. Explain that the written notes are for their own use - no-one else will see them as the game will be played verbally. You will need to provide encouragement as not many of us are very good at stressing our good points.

Now ask for a volunteer to begin by describing their five best points, together with examples. Make a contract with the group that everyone's input is to be heard in silence with no comments being made until everyone has had a go. Be sure to provide plenty of positive encouragement as group leader when people are making their inputs - some may be initially embarrassed at having to 'blow their own trumpet.'

Once the sequence has been completed, discussion can be invited on issues such as:

- Did you find out anything new about people?
- Did you find out anything which surprised you?
- How did the game make you feel?
- Is it a good thing to talk about our good points with others?

GUESS MY NAME

You should use this enjoyable game with a group of up to fifteen or so players who know one another fairly well. It is slightly similar to 'Chinese Roulette,' which we described in the *New Youth Games Book.* First of all have everyone write their name on a slip of paper. Now collect all the papers and mix them up well before inviting each person to choose a name. They should not disclose the name on their slip of paper to anyone else in the group.

One person should then volunteer to start the sequence off by making statements about the person named on their slip. These statements must be in the *first* person, e.g.
'I am.......'
'My favourite food is.....'
'I like to......'
'I enjoy.....'

The group should be invited to guess who this person is and the sequence then passes to the next person.

MESSAGES

With an advanced group where the members know one another well, you will probably want to encourage individuals to give personal feedback to one another. While this can at times be a painful process it is essential for group and personal development. In order to grow in our relationships with one another, we must practise the skill of providing honest, constructive feedback.

We stress that this kind of feedback technique must only be used where the group has already built up a fairly high level of trust. You will probably have used a number of physical trust exercises with your group and a number of more challenging games such as those suggested in the 'heavy end' section of the *New Youth Games Book.*

This particular exercise works best with a small group of eight people or less. Explain to the group that in order to learn to get on even better with one another, it is helpful to share information about things that we like and dislike about our individual behaviour in the group.

Now distribute copies of the 'message sheet' to group members and ask them to complete a sheet for *every* person in the group. Allow perhaps 10 to 20 minutes for this and encourage them to think carefully about the comments they want to make.

As leader, you should give some thought to the way you want to handle the feedback element of the exercise. The way you choose to handle this will affect the intensity of the exercise and the amount of time it takes to complete. Remember, too, that with this kind of trust activity it is essential that adults involved in the group participate as well - so prepare your adult helpers to be commented on!

(I)   The group leader collects all the 'message sheets' and sorts them into piles - they can then be fed back to each individual by the leader. This style of feedback *can* be kept anonymous, i.e. no mention of who said what to whom. Clearly, if a discussion follows the feedback on each individual, then it is open to people to declare the nature of their own comments. This is something the group leader will probably want to encourage as a 'good thing', but it is always useful to have a mechanism which enables people to have a 'let out.'

(ii)   The leader asks members to give their sheets to the appropriate person, so everyone ends up with seven or eight sheets. Allow a few minutes for the group to read the comments made about them and then ask for a volunteer to start off by responding to the comments from each group member. The volunteer should state to each person whether they are prepared to try to carry out their suggestions. The process should then continue around the group so that everyone has the opportunity to comment on their 'message sheets'. The session can be rounded off with a general discussion on the kinds of behaviour change requested by people, perhaps highlighting and discussing common issues. This style of feedback can be time consuming and intense, with the whole process taking between an hour and an hour and a half.

MESSAGE SHEET

From: .... **To:** ....

1.   I like it when you do these things ....

        Please keep doing them.

2.   Please do more of the following ....

3.   Please do less of these things ......

4.   Please think about starting to do these things ....

PASS THE SQUEEZE - variation

We have encouraged you elsewhere in this book to think about adapting games for your own particular purposes. We also think that it is a good idea to use games techniques for some of the everyday occurrences and organisational tasks in group life, e.g. selecting a volunteer, or splitting the group into pairs.

Clearly, this can become tiresome if over-used and we are not suggesting that you always use such techniques. However, with younger groups in particular, you will find a readiness to get involved. This variation of 'Pass the Squeeze' is an excellent example of:

- a simple variation of a technique
- using a technique for a different purpose
- incorporating a new technique into group culture.

Howie's daughter, Janey, was 'sold' on it by the 1st Brownies Pack, Peebles. This is what she wrote:

"You have a pretend squeeze in your hand. Then you pass it on. And then you tell the other person when you want to stop. Then it goes round the circle to the person; and then the person has to do a good and helpful thing at school or at home. So I did this game; by Janey Armstrong, age seven."

You can probably get the drift of how it is used from Janey's description. What fascinated us was how the technique had been adapted and incorporated into the week to week life of the group - they appear to use it each and every week, and of course, using it simply as a selection device means that it takes literally less than a minute to play.

To re-cap, the group leader sends a squeeze off around the circle (or nominates someone else to send it). The leader should close their eyes and then shout 'stop!' after a few seconds. The person who has the squeeze is then asked to do a helpful thing at home or school and report it back to the group the following week.

OFF YOUR CHEST

This is a useful exercise in encouraging the group to express a collective concern or emotion. It works particularly well where group members are uneasy or annoyed. We use this technique mainly with teenagers. As with many of these sequences, it is very important that the adult group leader is willing to participate in the sequence, thereby showing that there is *real* trust in the group.

Have the group sit in a circle and explain that they are going to collectively make some sort of statement - but each person can only contribute a word at a time! Explain that one person starts off with the first word of a sentence, and then the person on their left adds another and so on, right round the circle. Stress that the each word should follow on from the previous one.

This can be an interesting way of exposing 'hidden agendas,' and you may well be surprised to find out some of the preoccupations of your group. Obviously, watch out for individuals who cop out by only using expletives!

STATEMENTS

This is another one of these sequences which can be adapted for use at various stages of the group's development. It can be used with most sizes of group and can be very useful as an 'icebreaker' in the early stages of group development.

The technique tests individuals' knowledge of issues of importance to them and also invites them to make open ended statements about aspects of their lives. It is an ideal way of getting across information on children's rights, and you may want to use some of these publications for source material, but make sure that they are up to date:

Peter Jenkins, Children's Rights - A participative exercise for learning about children's rights in England and Wales. Longman. 1993.
Kathleen Murray, Children's rights in the Scottish context. National Children's Bureau (Scottish Group). 1987.
U.N. Convention on the Rights of the Child. 1989.

The questions you use should be tailored for your own particular legal environment, e.g. Scotland/England/Ireland.

The statements should be prepared on cards - 4 or 5 for each person, along the lines of:

You cannot be charged with an offence if you are under 8 years old.   *....True/False*

The time of day I like best is ....

The police cannot arrest you without informing your parents.   *.....True/False*

I like my best friend because ....

You can go to prison for not paying a fine.   *....True/False*

My ideal holiday would be ....

> If you tell a social worker something in confidence, they can't tell anyone else.
> ....True/False

> My best times at school are when ....

> The police can stop and search you without having a reason.
> ....True/False

The group should be seated in a circle for this game. Make sure that the cards have been well shuffled and ask someone to deal out 3 or 4 cards to each person. The remaining cards should be placed face down in the middle of the circle.

Players take it in turn to play one of their cards by giving the True/False answer or completing the sentence. Wrong True/False answers should be corrected, and discussed with the group if this seems appropriate. If someone can't play a card they miss a turn. However, a card can always be exchanged for one in the pile in the middle of the circle. The game ends when all cards have been played.

'Statements' can be very useful in developing the group's knowledge about children's rights. Typically, quite a few people (including adults!) will be surprised by some of the answers and these issues in particular can often lead into interesting discussions on some of the complexities of the legal system as it affects young people.

In the later stages of group development the 'open-ended' questions can be substituted for 'situations' ones, along the lines of:

> If I was asked to move on by the Police when I wasn't doing anything wrong, I would ....

> If my best friend started going out with my girl/boyfriend, I would ....

> If I found £10 in the street, I would ....

> If I wanted to go ice skating, but no-one else did, I would ....

With this version, encourage the group to comment on the appropriateness of responses to the 'situations' cards. Clearly, few of them will have right or wrong answers but the group will usually be able to come to a consensus view. It is always worth pointing out to the group that their consensus view may not be shared by teachers, social workers, court officials, police, etc.. Do they know what their views are and why they hold them? Again, interesting discussion can develop from some of these cards and you may wish to take some of the more interesting situations further through the use of other techniques, e.g. rôle play.

YOUR NUMBER'S UP

This is a useful exercise for developing non-verbal communication skills. You'll need pieces of card or paper, numbered according to how many participants you have in your group. So, for a group of 20 people, you'll need pieces of paper numbered 1-20. Put them in a container of some sort.

The group should be seated in a circle with one volunteer in the middle who will start the sequence off. All players in the circle should take a number from the container, without letting anyone else see it. You can now ask the volunteer to start by calling out a number (from 1-20 in this particular group). The person whose number has been called now calls out two different numbers - say 5 and 10. The holders of these two numbers must try to swap places - while the volunteer in the middle tries to snaffle one of their seats.

Of course, because players 5 and 10 don't know each others numbers, they must try to find and communicate with one another without the person in the middle noticing! If the person in the middle is successful in pinching a seat, then the person who lost their place must go in the middle. (Have the 'loser' give their number to the person leaving the centre so that they can participate in the game).

TELL ME TRUE

This is best used with a group where a degree of trust has already been established among group members. It works best with groups of up to fifteen people. As preparation you will need to write each group member's name on a piece of paper or card - and mix them up well prior to inviting each player to take one.

Now explain that everyone must write down at least three impressions they have of the person who is named on their piece of paper. Once everyone has finished, the papers are collected in and shuffled. They are then read out in turn, with the person who has been described trying to guess who wrote the impressions.

This exercise is useful in ascertaining attitudes towards one another amongst group members, and can be used to develop a discussion around ways in which we criticise one another. Since you are using this technique with an established group you would hope that criticisms aired (if any!) are done so in a constructive way, enabling you to stress the importance of this, if people are to feel able to take personal criticisms on board.

LIKES AND DISLIKES

This is a useful mechanism for encouraging reflection about people's perceptions of the group. It is a very simple technique which can be used at various stages of the group's development - in this way you can keep tabs on how people's perceptions are changing (or otherwise!).

The exercise works best with a small group of up to ten or twelve people. Everyone will need a pen or pencil and some paper. Simply ask each individual to list around five items that they like about the group, and five that they dislike.

A good way of taking the feedback from this exercise is to use a flipchart to score how many times a particular issue arises. Ask for a volunteer to start by reading out their likes and dislikes and write these issues up on the flipchart. Now as you go round the group asking for their issues, you can add new ones to the flipchart list and simply add a tick for repeated items.

At the end of the process you will have a 'snapshot' of how the group is perceived at this point in time. You can now invite discussion on the 'snapshot' view. For example, are there more dislikes than likes? Is there a shared view of the group, or does everyone have different likes and dislikes?

You can vary this technique as you wish in order to help your group look at other aspects of their lives, e.g. school, youth club, life at home, friends etc..

CHINESE WHISPERS

As old as the hills and needing little in the way of introduction, who knows where 'Chinese Whispers' originated? One theory is that it was so called in the First World War trenches, where messages transmitted from person to person down the line got more and more unintelligible along the chain of command. The classic example was *"Send re-inforcements, we're going to advance"* which became *"Send three and fourpence, we're going to a dance."* We've found this to be a little gem which is always entertaining, and can also be used to get a serious message across about the ways in which communication can go wrong.

'Chinese Whispers' can be used with any size of group but is most entertaining with larger numbers. The group should be seated in a circle, the task being to pass a (whispered) message from one person to the next until it has passed right round the group. Of course, when the last person to receive the message announces it to the group, the message usually bears little resemblance to the original one (if anyone can actually remember it!). This is one of these 'feel good' activities where every one has a tremendous laugh together at nobody else's expense.

Bear in mind that the most suitable messages contain more than a couple of words; while the message shouldn't be unduly complex it must have several elements so that it will inevitably become 'corrupted' as it is passed round a fifteen strong group! An example might be: *"meet me to-morrow afternoon at half past three outside Alistair's shop - and don't forget your skates and the 23p you owe me."*

Of course if you choose to de-brief this exercise, rather than simply playing it for fun, a number of interesting points can be made. For example, it should be obvious that the more people involved in transmitting a message the higher the likelihood of error - this explains why rumours often bear little resemblance to the original issue. 'Chinese Whispers' also demonstrates why it is so dangerous to accept 'hearsay' opinion about people and things - much better to get your information from the horse's mouth if at all possible.

BIRTHDAY PRESENT

This fun sequence falls into the 'wishful thinking' category. It is suitable for a group of up to eight or so members, and no equipment is needed.

Begin the sequence by asking for a volunteer who will have an imaginary birthday. Now, starting with one of the players sitting next to the volunteer each person takes it in turn to state what birthday present they would give to the volunteer. Encourage inventive thinking here, with no restrictions as to the amount of money available for present buying. With an advanced group, you may want to have people think in terms of personal qualities which could be given, rather than physical presents.

Once everyone has stated the nature of their gift, the volunteer has to decide which present they would like - only one is allowed. The player whose gift is accepted has the next birthday, and the sequence continues.

ACTIVE LISTENING

This is one of the most important relationship skills young people can ever learn. Introduce the exercise by sharing how you feel when not being listened to, e.g. when the person you are talking to fidgets with the papers on their desk and obviously can't wait to get rid of you.

In this exercise we concentrate on non-verbal messages, rather than more obvious verbal 'put downs'. We usually play this in 'triads' - groups of three, with one talker, one listener, and an observer to provide feedback. Each group of three should be seated so that the talker and listener are facing each other, with the observer sitting to one side but with a clear view of the other two.

Stage one: brief the listener to provide plenty of positive non-verbal feedback to the talker, e.g. regular eye contact, nods of the head, quiet sounds of affirmation (hmm, hmm) etc.. The talker should be asked to speak for a couple of minutes on any topic they wish while the observer should be asked to take note of the general situation, and in particular how the talker appears to react as a result of the listener's non-verbal communications.

Stage two: this time, brief the listener to make their non-verbal gestures negative ones, e.g. minimum eye contact, looking away or out of the window, fidgeting, distracting by dropping a pencil, etc..

Stage three: ask the members of each triad to swap places and run the sequence twice more. This ensures that everyone has experienced the three roles of talker, listener and observer.

Stage four: invite each triad to debrief; first of all by discussing how different it felt for the talker when they had an *active* listener rather than a disinterested one.

Stage five: bring the whole group together for a more general debriefing. Points which can usefully be teased out include that having an active listener can help the talker to provide a fuller 'story' - i.e. if your listener is actively providing encouragement and showing interest, then as a talker you are all the more likely to *want to tell* your story, to get it across to someone who is interested and obviously wants to hear it. Also, when a listener is active they are much more likely to be paying attention and *really* listening. Finally, was the observer role helpful in highlighting for people what was *actually* going on - sometimes rather different from what they thought was happening?

SEX ROLES

Ideal for mixed older groups who know one another well, this technique is designed to help young people look at sex role stereotypes. It would be best used in the context of a social education group looking at sex education or relationships. Suitable for groups of up to twenty people, you will need some paper and pens.

Split your group into male and female sub groups and ask them to discuss the following two questions:

> - What is typically feminine behaviour?
>
> - What is typically masculine behaviour?

Depending on how involved the young people are in the discussion, allow up to 30 minutes for this. Ask each group to write down their thoughts so that they can provide feedback. Now bring the groups back together again to hear feedback from the sub groups. After hearing the feedback ask the group:

> - Was there agreement in each group as to typical sex roles?
>
> - Did the male and female groups reach the same, or different conclusions?
>
> - Were any of the sex roles thought to be unhelpful?
>
> - Can we do without, or change, these sex roles?

After this discussion ask for two female and two male volunteers to perform a short rôle-play. This should be a typical everyday scene, e.g. chatting in the school playground, having a coke in the youth club. The twist is that the girls must pretend to be boys and vice versa!

It is likely that the rôle-play will bring out aspects of sex role prejudice and stereotyping. Finish the session off by asking small mixed groups to discuss these issues and then feedback in the large group.

CATCH ME IF YOU CAN

This can be quite an energetic sequence, and involves a bit of running so make sure that there are no obstructions around. Any size of group from eight people upwards can be involved and no equipment is needed, but you do require quite a lot of space.

Begin by having the group stand in a circle which is fairly well spaced out - about five feet between each person. Now ask the group to walk around in their circle - without changing the size of the circle. Once people are used to this, ask them to try to keep as close as possible to the person in front of them without actually touching that person. This should cause the group to run at a fair old speed around the circle.

Now introduce the 'catch me' command, at which point all the players must try to catch up with the person in front and touch their back. Of course, they must try to do this while avoiding having their own back touched by the person behind them! This is an interesting 'filler' type of exercise which takes only a couple of minutes to play.

HUMAN TRAIN

This is a trust sequence involving participants being blindfolded (or agreeing to keep eyes shut). As such, the leader should outline the usual safety considerations. You will need a fairly large playing area, such as a games hall or a recreation field, and you should have a number of helpers around to prevent players bumping into walls, obstructions etc.. This sequence is suitable for all ages and numbers up to fifteen or so.

Have the players form a 'human train' by lining up behind one another and holding onto the shoulders or waist of the person in front. Everyone should be blindfold, or have eyes shut *except* for the player at the front of the train. This person's task is to lead the others around the playing area negotiating obstacles by stepping over or around them, crouching down to go underneath them, over the top or whatever.

The lead player may signal the existence and type of obstacle to the others by signalling to the person immediately behind, who then passes the signal on. Only touch signals are allowed and you should therefore ask the lead player, at the beginning of the sequence, to identify the signals and communicate them to the rest of the group.

It's best not to use this sequence for too long a time, as people find that being blindfold while moving around can be quite a strain

As well as being an interesting trust exercise, it also can help introduce a group to questions about disabilities.

PHRASES

Word games of various sorts are numerous, as are treasure hunt games. 'Phrases' is a mixture of both. The organiser needs to prepare both a set of phrases on an answer sheet and a set of numbered cards with numbered key words which act as clues. The way we play the game is similar to how Robin Dynes uses his version.

We distribute the 'key word' cards around the room, usually face down on table tops round the edge of the room. Everyone in the room is then invited to turn over cards and then talk to other people about what well-known phrase might use the object named on the card. The aim is that 'Phrases' should be a co-operative group activity. It works well with younger adolescent groups and can usually take about quarter of an hour to twenty minutes. After about eight or ten minutes of group activity round the cards, ask the group to collect up the cards from the tables. Then the organiser can call out the words on the cards and see what phrases the group members have come up with. Unlike, Robin, we have tended to use this without scoring individuals.

The following cards and their related phrases are offered as examples of how the game works:

CARD OBJECT	PHRASE
1. Ice	As cold as ice
2. Night	As black as night
3. Feather	As light as a feather
4. Barn	Born in a barn
5. Snow	As soft as snow
6. Pot	Pot calling the kettle black
7. Picture	As pretty as a picture
8. Heart	Heart of darkness
9. Broom	New broom sweeps clean
10. Rat	To smell a rat

As you prepare the cards and match them to the numbered phrases, you'll find some that may have more than one answer. For instance, 'pot' can also fit: 'to keep the pot boiling'. This doesn't matter. The aim is to provide a bit of creativity.

COMMENTS

Use this sequence at the end of a session as a means of encouraging the group to give feedback to one another. You will need a number of prepared cards like:

- I enjoyed myself when .....

- I didn't like .....

- It was a good laugh when .....

- The most interesting thing I did was .....

- The funniest thing was .....

- The thing which interested me least was .....

- I would like to do more of .....

- I would like to do less of .....

- The person who has been a
  good friend is .....

- I was most angry when .....

- What I learned about myself was .....

  - I was upset when .....

  - I was happy when .....

  - I was nervous when .....

- The person who was kindest to me is .....

  - My best memory is .....

- The thing I most disliked was .....

The group should be sitting in a circle with the cards placed face down in the middle. Explain that each person has to take a card and answer it as honestly as possible. Stress that the answers should apply to this group session only. Allow questions to be asked after each person has answered their card - some people may not have witnessed the situation being referred to.

This can be a challenging technique, particularly with a group where people know each other well, as dishonest answers are likely to be spotted immediately and taken up. Make sure that everyone takes a turn.

SPEAKEASY

We're not exactly sure where this one originated! Certainly, it's a variation of the 'Computer' game in the *New Youth Games Book.* We do know that it was being used by IT workers in Strathclyde Region in 1988. Games aficionados will know that 'Computer' is one of the most popular relationship games of all time with young people - they never seem to tire of it.

In many senses, 'Speakeasy' is like an advanced tailor-made version of 'Computer.' The game is designed to encourage group members to notice important details about each other; also, it is structured to help young people talk to, and about, one another.

Like 'Computer,' this game uses cards and these must be prepared in advance. The cards need to be written with specific group members in mind, so you need to make sure that there are cards for every group member, including adults. Aim to have at least four or five cards for each person. Cards might include:

- Got much more involved in group activities this week
- Was winding people up tonight
- Seems to be happier at school now
- Volunteered to make supper tonight
- Didn't clear up after woodwork
- Annoyed people tonight by slagging them off

This technique works well with a small group - maximum group size is about fourteen. Everyone should be seated in a circle and a volunteer chosen to shuffle and deal the cards. The cards should be dealt face down - three to each person, with the remainder placed face down in the middle of the group.

Each player takes it in turn to play a card. They choose one of their three cards and decide to whom it is most appropriate to give it. The giving of the card **must** be accompanied by a specific statement in evidence, e.g. "I am giving you this card because I noticed that you didn't clear up after woodwork tonight" - the card can now be passed to that person.

You can allow people to 'pass' if, for example, they can't think of the right person to give the card to, or think that the cards they hold are too 'difficult.' However, although 'passes' should always be allowed with this kind of exercise, players can be encouraged to swap one of their cards for one from the central pile so that they can make a play.

The sequence is played until everyone has given over their three cards. At this point, assuming that the cards have been well prepared and the game has been played honestly, everyone should have been given a few cards during the process of the game. Of course, adults involved in the game will have been at pains to make sure that the game has been played fairly and that every player has been given some cards.

To round off the sequence invite people to comment on the cards they have been given.

'Speakeasy' is an excellent way of encouraging young people to offer positive and negative feedback to one another. Issues to bring out include: that everyone has their bad points as well as good ones, and that even a bad week will have something good about it.

ESCAPE
We have adapted this challenging exercise from Sue Jennings' 'Creative Drama in Groupwork.' The group does not need any equipment for this exercise, apart from their own imagination. It works best with half a dozen people, so a large group should be split up, and the experiences compared at the end.

Explain to the group that while away on a weekend camp they have managed to lock themselves into a wooden hut in the middle of a forest. It is beginning to get dark and they are all hungry so they really need to hatch an immediate escape plan.

The main problem is that the road they used to get to the hut has been blocked by a landslide and they will need to take another route. In order to effect their escape the group will need to:

- break out of the hut
- climb a 15 foot wall
- get over a 6 foot barbed wire fence
- cross a river
- cross some very boggy ground.

The group must try to reach agreement on what *three* things (pieces of equipment) would be most useful to aid an escape.

DEMO

The scene is an animal rights demonstration where the police are threatening to arrest one of the demonstrators who has been very vocal (but non violent). A small group of eight to ten people should be asked to rôle play this scenario in an attempt to resolve it. In a larger group the remaining members can act as spectators.

Take care to brief the group that the scenario should not be allowed to get too out of hand, i.e. no actual physical violence against one another etc.. In debriefing this exercise you will want to tease out whether there was any serious attempt (by either side) to defuse the situation and solve it constructively - or whether people simply attack and insult each other. Also important is whether there was any expressed sympathy for one another's positions.

If the 'animal rights' setting does not seem appropriate, design one which is more suitable for your group, such as:

- a fight between two sets of football fans with police involved;
- Travellers who are parked up with their families being evicted by the council and police;
- a British Movement/National Front march through a predominantly Asian neighbourhood.

IMPROVISE

This is a useful technique to use as a 'spectator' event with a large group of twelve or more. As the title suggests, it challenges people to improvise a short dramatic scene. Players are given a starting point and must work together to complete the scenario.

You will need a number of cards with the starting points written on them. They could be along the lines of:

- The janitor/caretaker was walking across the playground. Just then ....

- The policemen turned the corner and walked towards the young people when ....

- Tom and Joe were kicking the football to each other. Suddenly ....

- Mary was just dropping off to sleep when ....

- David had just managed to get the cat down from the tree and ....

You will only need one or two cards for every three or four people in your group. Now split the group up into smaller groups of three or four and get each group to choose a card at random. Explain that they have to improvise what happened after the initial scene outlined on the card. Invite the groups to leave the room, or go into a quiet corner to plan out their improvisation - allow only about four or five minutes planning time as you are not expecting sophisticated dramatic presentations.

Now bring the whole group back together again and form them into a circle. Invite each group in turn to make their presentations. Provide plenty of encouragement to the groups as they present their improvisation, particularly if it is the first time they have tackled an exercise like this. As groups perform, you can encourage the others to guess what the scenario is about. Make sure that each group receives applause after they finish.

'Improvise' can lead to some very funny scenarios being created. It is a useful exercise for increasing self confidence and encouraging collaborative working.

RIVERS

This paper and pencil game is played in many countries - Mihai and Radu from Romania reminded us of it. It can be played with any size of group, but it involves some writing so you should make sure that all your group members have basic writing skills. It is also an alternative to 'Guggenheim' described earlier in this chapter and the commercially available game called 'Tell Me.'

Each person should have paper and pencil, with the paper ruled off in columns headed up 'Rivers', 'Countries', 'Towns', Plants' or anything else you or your group decide. One person is chosen to begin reciting the alphabet (again, you should check that your players can actually do this!). At some point at random during the recitation, say after the letter 'R' the person says 'start.' Each individual in the group then has two or three minutes to write down a river, country, town etc. beginning with the letter 'R'.

The sequence then continues with the person to the left of the original caller reciting the alphabet and stopping at another letter. The same letter can be repeated, but players then have to think of different names beginning with that letter. After about ten letters have been played, the sheets should be scored with one point being given for each correct name and two points for correct names when a letter has been repeated.

ROMANIA/BULGARIA

Radu Sabau was enthusiastic about this active ball game played in his native Romania. This is another energetic activity ideal for a small group of seven to ten participants. Play starts from a circle in the centre of the playing area which should be marked out in half a dozen or so segments. Each segment is allocated to a particular country, e.g. Romania, Bulgaria, USA, France, Britain etc.

Play begins with a player in each segment with one foot in their own segment and the other foot outside the circle. In the centre of the circle is a player (caller) with the soft ball. The aim of the game is to be the last person (country) to be eliminated.

Play commences with the caller throwing the ball high into the air from the centre of the circle and calling out the name of a country, e.g. Bulgaria. 'Bulgaria' must try to catch the ball before it lands, and all other players run as far as they can from the circle before Bulgaria shouts 'Stop!'. All players must instantly stop on the spot and Bulgaria now has one throw to try to hit another player to eliminate them from the game.

If a player is hit, then they and their country are out of the game and the sequence continues with another throw and call from the centre spot- minus Bulgaria. The caller does not have things all their own way, however, as if they call an 'out' country later on in the game, then they are out and the sequence finishes.

TRIPLE NAMES

A simple sequence for younger groups to help them remember the names of all the group members. The group should be standing or sitting in a circle. One person is chosen to begin the sequence by repeating their own name three times and then naming someone else in the group, e.g.

> 'Howie, Howie, Howie, **Alan.**'

At the same time everyone makes a rhythmic 'pushing' movement with both hands held out in front of them. If your group is in a noisy mood you can use hand claps instead.

The newly named person then continues the sequence by repeating their own name three times and then adding another group member's name, e.g.

> 'Alan, Alan, Alan, **Julie.**'

Younger groups love this sequence because of the rhythm and repetition. As group leader you should encourage people to get into a nice steady rhythm.

PARTISAN

We include this energetic ball game here because it can be played with as few as eight people and is useful in encouraging groups to think about team-building strategies. The game is played with a soft ball and you will need access to an indoor or outdoor playing court. This should be marked out in two halves with a 'throwing strip' of a few feet in width at each end of the pitch.

We know that 'Partisan' is played in Romania - Mihai Rosca told us of it one night after a folk concert of traditional music in neighbouring Sofia. Mihai is one of the few people we have met who has moved from medicine to youth social work, although this sort of career move is not uncommon in Eastern Europe due to very strange salary differentials (e.g. taxi drivers earning more than doctors in some cases).

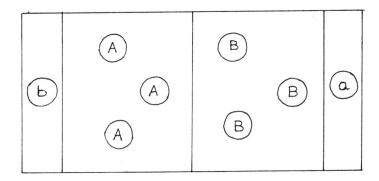

The two teams for the game are made up of three or four players and they can move freely around their own half of the court. An additional player from each team is allowed to occupy the 'throwing strip' *behind* the opposing team. Teams should toss a coin to decide who throws first. If we call our teams A and B, as in the diagram, it is the 'a' or 'b' player who throws first, i.e. one of those occupying the throwing strips.

The aim is to eliminate players from the opposing team by hitting them with the ball. So , if 'a' say, throws and hits a member of the B team, then that team member is out of the game. If, however, the B team member manages to catch the ball, they can throw it directly at the A team. When a player is ruled out, the throw goes to the line thrower of the opposing team.

'Partisan' can be a very exciting and fast moving sequence, well worthy of introducing your group to. The teambuilding element comes from involving your group in thinking about who possesses the specific skills needed to excel in the roles of thrower and catcher. Hopefully, your group can learn that fielding their most accurate thrower in the throwing role, together with a few rounds practice, can produce a cracking team.

WHAT'S YOUR NAME - LEMONADE!

This is one of these sequences which children love, as it involves rhyme, rhythm, repetition..... and shouting. Larger groups are best for this sequence - about sixteen people upwards. The group should be split into two and one group is sent into a huddle to decide *as a group* on:

- their trade, e.g. plumber, farmer, teacher and how they will mime it;
- their name;
- where they come from.

The two teams then line up facing one another, and about twenty feet apart. We can call the teams the 'traders' (those who decided on their trade, name etc.) and the questioners.

At a signal from the games leader, the questioners all take a big step forward and shout, *'What's your name?'* The traders all take a big step forward and reply with their agreed name. The questioners now take another giant step forward and shout *'Where do you come from?'* Again, the traders take a giant step towards the questioners and reply with their agreed town or city. Finally, the questioners take another step forward and shout *'What's your trade?'* The traders take a step forward and reply, *'LEMONADE!'* At the same time they all do a little mime of what their trade is.

The questioners now have to guess what the trade is, and anyone who thinks they know the answer shouts it out. The traders must listen carefully to the shouted guesses, because as soon as a correct guess is made, the traders run away from the questioners who try to catch them. Any trader who is caught has to join the questioners' team and the sequence continues with the remaining traders getting into a huddle to decide on their new trade, with a new line up etc. The game finishes when all traders have been eliminated.

Claudia Beamish and Michael Derrington shared this game with us. They use it in their drama work with young people and at the many children's parties they host at Westraw House in Lanarkshire, Scotland.

COLD, WARM, HOT

We had almost forgotten about this simple game until reminded of it in Bulgaria, where it is popular with younger children. It is a perfect party game and we have even known adult groups to have had some fun with this one!

A volunteer is needed to leave the room while the group decides on a hiding place for an object. The volunteer is then invited back into the room and begins to search for the object. The group gives clues to the location of the object by shouting 'cold' if the volunteer is looking in the wrong place or heading in the wrong direction. 'Warm' is shouted if the direction is right or the volunteer is close to the object, and 'hot' if they are very close to it.

At a party, or if you need to increase motivation, the object can be a prize of a toy or sweet which is kept by the volunteer (if successful!).

FRANKENSTEIN

The excellent 'Communicado' theatre company use this game regularly as an icebreaker. You will need quite a large group for this - the more the merrier, as they say, but a minimum number of a dozen people.

Have your group spread out around the room and choose one person to be 'Frankenstein.' This person holds both arms out in front of them and moves slowly towards the other players. The other players *are not allowed to move!* Eye contact is a feature of this game, as Frankenstein attempts to terrify their victims into passive submission with their chilling gaze!

So, the scenario we have is Frankenstein, arms held out, choosing a victim by eye contact and moving slowly and inexorably towards them. Should Frankenstein actually manage to touch their victim, then that person becomes Frankenstein.

Now here comes the interesting bit. A victim can save themselves by shouting out someone else's name, turning that person into Frankenstein! So Frankenstein can pop up literally anywhere. Terrifying indeed!

A few words on strategy. To be most effective and terrifying, it is probably a good idea for Frankenstein to 'eyeball' the victim when only a few feet away from them - this gives the victim only a few seconds to think of another person's name and shout it out. However, if the victim names someone who is already out, then they themselves are out of the game. Note that there is only one Frankenstein operating at a time (thank goodness!) - as a victim shouts a name, that named person instantly becomes Frankenstein and the original Frankenstein becomes a player.

CAT AND MOUSE

With similarities to 'Escape/Outsider' from the New Youth Games Book, we liked this game given to us by Spaska Malinova from Velingrad in Bulgaria. 'Cat and Mouse' can be used with groups of ten people upwards.

You will need two volunteers for this sequence, and the rest of the group should be standing in a tight circle holding hands. One volunteer - the mouse - is inside the circle, with the other - the cat - outside the circle. The aim of the game is simple and obvious: the cat has to try to break in to the circle to catch the mouse, and the group members forming the circle have to prevent the cat getting in.

All the while the cat is trying to break in, the circle moves round. This makes the whole sequence quite lively and affords the cat a number of strategies for breaking through, e.g. trying to wriggle through moving legs, watching carefully for a gap to appear as the circle moves round. If the mouse is caught, it joins the circle and the cat becomes the new mouse. A new volunteer is needed to become the cat outside the circle and the game can continue.

In Bulgaria they sing a little song as they play this game:

'At home we have a mouse eating cheese,
The cat wants to eat the mouse,
Run! Run! mouse, the cat wants to eat you'.

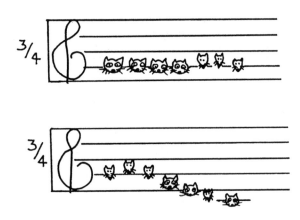

As with 'Escape/Outsider' you can run the sequence first of all with the group facing inwards towards the centre of the circle, and then facing out. Debriefing can be used to determine how the cat felt when the group was facing them rather than with backs to them. Also, is it more difficult for the cat to break in when it can be seen by the group, i.e. when they are facing outwards?

HARLEM SHUFFLE

This is a nice little co-operative sequence which is especially good with younger children. It is an ideal icebreaker, or can be used as an ending sequence, to send everyone in the group home in a good mood!

The group organiser asks everyone to sort themselves out into straight lines, with five people in each. This is done quickly. The organiser now says:
> "Close your eyes."

All the people in the lines are now shuffled around with their eyes closed, so that they have moved into a different line and in a strange position. When the organiser now asks them:
> "Sort yourselves out."

This is the invitation for everyone in the group to open their eyes and work together to get themselves back to their original starting positions.

BACK DANCE

You need a cassette recorder, CD, musical instrument, radio or something which can produce music to run this quick, fun sequence. Again, it is designed to help young people relax together and overcome inhibitions. In a mixed group it is nice to get boys and girls dancing together - but it is dancing with a definite twist!

The organiser asks everyone to pair up, then asks them to join together linking up their arms so their backs are touching. At the commencement of the music all the couples should start dancing around, keeping themselves joined together until the music stops. It certainly gives everyone a good opportunity to look at other people's partners.....

If you want to prolong the sequence, get the pairs to change partners two or three times.

INDEX

INDEX

A Few Card Games....30

About Me....99

Active Listening....122

Adverts....110

Aeroplane....59

Affirmation Rounds....111

Alan's Hunt....69

All Stand...108

April Fools' Games....59

Art Arena Games....86

Awari....50

Back Dance....136

Back to Back Race 83

Battling Tops....61

Beetle....16

Bell Toss....56

Bert's Gate....38

Birthday Present....122

Black....8

Blind Run....105

Bonus Point Scrabble....52

Bottle Toss....92

Brother Jonathan....91

Bump Tag....79

Caroms....44

Cat and Mouse....135

Catch Me if You Can...124

Characteristics....101

Chase Games....78

Chinese Whispers....121

Coin Throwing....91

Cold, Warm, Hot....134

Comments....126

Connections....106

Crag....18

Crows and Cranes....79

Curved Ball....54

Deck Quoits....78

Demo....129

Dice Games....15

Dictionary Game....48

Dots and Lines....38

Dotty....25

Double Bag Scrabble....52

Dreidles....19

Escape....128

Eskimo House....65

Fan Tan....10

Fighting Kites....66

Fishy Match....25

Five of the Best....113

Five Start Scrabble....51

Forehead Game....8

Frankenstein....134

French Cricket....88

Frog or Rabbit Race....84

Game of Books....36

Getting to Know You....108

Glass Trick....23

Go Boom....32

Gooly-Dunda....58

Greek Ball....89

Guess my Name....113

Guggenheim....102

Hand Games....33

Happy Families....31

Harlem Shuffle....136

Hash Running....73

Hearts....19

Hei Tama tu Tama....33

Hoop Race....83

Hoppy Currie....85

Hopscotch....58

Horseshoes....77

How to use this book....4

Human Train....125

Improvise....130

Introduction....2

Inventing a Game....38

Jeu de Boules....92

Jewish Passover: Festival of
  Freedom....52

July 4th Celebration Games....56

Kabaddi....70

Kick the Can....88

Knee Bends....23

Lateral Problem....26

Le Vieux Garcon....31

Likes and Dislikes....120

Longy-della....79

Major benefits from use of
  games....3

Mancala Games....50

Martinetti....17

Match This....26

Messages....114

Mime Challenge....110

Mind Game....107

Monsters....80

Moon....65

Nigel's Hunt....69

Nikitin Materials....12

Number Pairs....34

Odd Art Competition....60

Off your Chest....116

Old and Antique Board & Table
  Games....21

Organisation of this book....6

Other ideas for Races....84

Pachisi....35

Pack your Bag....112

Pairs....99

Palindromes....24

Partisan....132

Pass the Squeeze - variation....115

Penny on the Drum....91

Personal Shields....109

Picture Pairs....100

Piggyback Tag....79

Pigs can Fly.....61

Planks....47

Planning for games sessions....5

Playing Cards....26

Polish Draughts....9

Post Office Balls....68

Problems....105

Pulling the Rod....90

Put and Take....11

Puzzle Time....23

Queeny, Kingy or Tag ball....81

Quoits and Horseshoes....76

Quoits....76

Recycler Scrabble....52

Red Rover....80

Relationship games
   introduction....96

Ringboard....21

Ring Games....20

Rivers....130

Romania/Bulgaria....131

Scavenger Hunt....83

Scrabble Variations....51

Sex Roles....123

Slapjack....30

Solo Scrabble....52

Speakeasy....127

Spellicans....44

Squails...46

Squeeze the Knee....104

Statements....117

States' Shuffleboard....57

Tangram....14

Tarrocco....28

Tell me True....120

The Fossil....59

Things with String....63

Three Way Tug of War....90

Tippet....34

Treasure Hunts....69

Triple Names....132

Up Jenkins....34

Wall Game....81

Weigh Butter....85

Weird Objects....61

Weird Races....82

What's your Name -
   Lemonade!....133

Who you can use the games with....4

Wordles....101

Your Number's up....119